THE L.A. COOKBOOK

ALISON CLARE STEINGOLD
PHOTOGRAPHS BY NOAH FECKS

THE L.A. COOKBOOK

RECIPES FROM THE BEST
RESTAURANTS, BAKERIES, AND BARS
IN LOS ANGELES

RIZZOLI
NEW YORK

New York · Paris · London · Milan

Dedicated to the next generation of Los Angeles chefs,
whoever and wherever you are.

First published in the United States of America in 2018
by Rizzoli International Publications, Inc.
300 Park Avenue South
New York, NY 10010
www.rizzoliusa.com

Photographs © Noah Fecks
noahfecks.com

Case and interior design by Jeri Heiden and Nick Steinhardt for SMOG Design, Inc.
smogdesign.com

2022 2023 2024 2025 / 10 9 8 7 6

Distributed to the U.S. trade by Random House, New York
Printed in China

ISBN-13: 978-0-8478-6167-5

Library of Congress Catalog Control Number: 2017948438

CONTENTS

INTRODUCTION

Let's retire those old L.A. jabs about new-age cafes serving alfalfa and plates of mashed yeast. Los Angeles has arrived.

Here, chefs are popping up, settling down, tending the hearth, and foraging in the field. Yet, however distinguished the individual accolades, they've rarely been recognized as a whole. *The L.A. Cookbook* hopes to cut through the smog of outdated cliché and reveal a modern food capital having its moment. Sure, the California dream forever lingers like haze with all its attendant beauty, stardom, and sunshine. Behind that illusion, though, there's a full-fledged culinary community to connect all of us, ground us, remind us who we are.

Lulled by the monotony of an endless supply of sunshine, Angelenos search for extremes on the periphery, and dining culture follows suit: brushfires, droughts, moody marine layers;

sticky baklava in Glendale, mouth-numbing pepper oil in Chinese Beverly Hills; super-sour umeboshi in Little Tokyo West. When fatigued by extremes, there's the burger, the taco—the 72-and-sunny comfort of L.A. cuisine.

In a journey sometimes raw, sometimes refined, and most often a little of both, this compendium adapts 100 of the city's most-wanted, exclusive, and hidden-gem recipes. Each has been vetted to reflect the compelling styles, ingredients, flavors, techniques, and ideas that make L.A. a dynamic global destination for food.

So before L.A. slides off into the Pacific, or before Hollywood swallows us up and spits us out, and before we consume our way through clothing and cars, cash and flash, these dishes share how we can all get *it*. It? That taste of L.A.

What Is "So L.A." Anyway?

You've got burgers, donuts, French dip, juice bars, raw vegan, Cobb salads, Shirley Temples, hot fudge sundaes, frozen yogurt, California rolls, even sriracha. Though pioneered in Los Angeles, what might have been deemed Los Angeles food has been co-opted as American trend, then adopted in diners and sushi houses coast to coast. To wit, Hollywood distributed the original brand of medication, and America pumped out the generic drug. Then what *is* Angelean food?

In her seminal history of California's food revolution in the 1970s, veteran chef/writer Joyce Goldstein takes a bold stance on "California" cuisine: "Unlike traditional cuisines, which have their roots in the home and community, California cuisine originated in restaurants," she writes. No one, she continues, would visit a friend's house for "California food" the way we might have a Spanish or Lebanese theme dinner party. It is a culture unto itself, a site-specific phenomenon, restaurant-born and bred.

How democratic, a sense of place! Show up, and you are free to learn to cook it, or to experience it like everyone else. L.A.'s proliferation of internationally specific eateries offers a kind of cultural exchange between tradition and innovation. As a magazine writer and editor of California food, wine, and dining for the past 14 years, I believe the word *access* best describes this thriving culture. Los Angeles sits in proximity to the freshest, most diverse produce; wee-hours fish markets to please even the most demanding sushi artisans; finest Thai and Korean markets this side of the Pacific; and a gargantuan port for any rare spice or undiscovered vegetable you can track down on Google.

KCRW "Good Food" host, chef, and all-around culinary doyenne Evan Kleiman crystallized the notion further in a 2008 Zócalo panel moderated by Jonathan Gold: "What our [L.A.'s] unique window into the world of food is these extraordinary diverse foods of the world, seen through the prism of California produce and other local ingredients," she says. "Our flavors tend to be brighter and clearer, and less muddy and more elegant. Flavors reveal themselves in a direct way."

In this book, each recipe represents a facet in the prism of influences, ingredients, techniques, and styles comprising the L.A. dishes you love while here and crave while away. Those facets help define what makes a dish "so L.A."

A Showcase for Ingredients

Seasonal California cooking tips its cap to the farmers and foragers in the 1970s who knocked on back doors of kitchens with never-before-seen produce; of chefs drafting daily menus worded to stoke a new kind of romance for a California terroir. Also during those early 1970s, when nouvelle cuisine was all the rage, many European chefs arrived in Los Angeles (Wolfgang Puck, Michel Richard, and Joachim Splichal among them). Young American chefs, in turn, traveled abroad and returned home with educated palates.

That California narrative has proven decisive. You could walk like a duck and talk like a duck, but if you couldn't understand *why* a Liberty Farms Duck was of value, well, you weren't tapped into the magic of this "California" food narrative. In other words: Without the backstory, you're missing the point. You're just eating duck.

As a result, the rise of ingredients-only lists on menus has downplayed technique and instead pushed a powerful shorthand into the spotlight. Homage to Escoffier and Larousse are no longer. Perhaps feeling fancy isn't necessarily what Angelenos are after. *De rigueur* 2018: farms, tradition, childhood favorites, and hyper-specific regions of cuisine that balances—the face-value paradox of rustic and refined.

As you cook through the book, you might find that the produce required to make a certain dish isn't in season. Welcome to market cooking's golden rule: Cook what's at peak. Let this idea embolden you to shop your regional produce utilizing similar logic.

A Melting Pot of Flavors

However apprehensive drivers are to merge on the 101, we haven't been so fearful in matters of merging foods. Los Angeles is an international city. There's a Model UN's worth of enclaves out here: Mexican, Filipino, Armenian, Thai, Greek, Chinese, Vietnamese, Japanese, Korean, Salvadoran, Brazilian, Ethiopian, Palestinian, Israeli, Persian, Russian . . . you name it. Whatever growing pains neighborhoods face—gentrification, urban sprawl, assimilation—they've worked syncretistic wonders for a population of 18 million in a system of curlicue arteries covering 4,850 square miles. Culinary

mashups such as Roy Choi's Kogi Korean BBQ tacos have shifted the tides of this food wave. To call it global or fusion or California cuisine doesn't cut it, but perhaps Angelean does.

Access has also increased exploration of niche global flavors. Thanks to the culinary megastore that is the internet, what seemed so exotic only a decade ago is reminiscent of teenagers listening to Elvis today and trying to understand why he was so edgy.

A Recontextualization of Tradition

Crafting new traditions out of old taps into the L.A. feeling with a new sincerity. Tradition places the onus on the chef, pushing dining as a chef-driven, personal, or generational expression of ideas on the plate. In line with L.A.'s cult of individuality, chefs are increasingly free to write their own rules. Here, they aren't captive to the "California cuisine" narrative. That seems to suit them just fine.

Bistronomy, the L.A. Way

In the past, if you had the grit to cook in a Michelin-worthy restaurant, you did. In 1990s Paris, top chefs and critics who were aghast by the notion of top chefs opening "casual" eateries began to embrace the bistro and its lush terrines, braised meats, and low-tech lifestyle. Eventually, Paris loosened up and gastronomy punched a special new hole in its belt.

L.A. was naturally drawn to the seeming juxtaposition: the more the casual concept contrasted the food, the more

we embraced it. Whereas precision and accuracy used to be the target in white-tablecloth fine dining, the objects of affection have changed. Aesthetics have changed. Diners now sit elbow-to-elbow at communal tables. Tall spires of gladiolus, are abandoned for local flowers and vertical greenery. Christofle silver and Bernardaud porcelain have been swapped for local ceramics and deliberately mismatched china. When they form a makeshift table and chair to devour your fennel salami pizza, a couple of devil-may-care GTA milk crates are nothing to sniff at.

Freedom from Kitchen Hierarchy

It isn't hyperbolic to say that the Great Recession resculpted L.A.'s culinary landscape. Beginning in 2008, a seeming disaster for fine-dining restaurants left many chefs unemployed. The forced closure of restaurants, end of three-martini lunches and big pharma buyouts and halt in construction meant layoffs. It disrupted the rigid chain of French-style kitchen command that rewarded veteran status. On the upside, cooks didn't have to be far into their careers before flying solo. Closed retailers and businesses meant vacant spaces, which meant a chef might just have a place, or truck, to rent for a month. Thanks to social media and a love for underdog tales of dream-seeking mavericks setting out on their own, these pop-ups, residencies, and food trucks became the future: Kogi, Alma, and Wolf in Sheep's Clothing.

That's the thing I respect most: L.A. moves forward, no matter the

circumstance. *The L.A. Cookbook* is one snapshot of that creativity.

Matt Molina of Everson Royce Bar frames the scene succinctly: "[L.A. restaurants are] like a broken nebula that went all over the place. . . . The whole allure of L.A. at this particular moment, being one of the hottest food cities in the U.S., is its unpredictability. You never know where it's going to go."

Creating Your L.A. Pantry

100 dishes from 100 chefs means 100 different styles of recipe. In this book, "adaptation" means to make them relatively consistent, in clear language across this diversity of voices with as little pretense and gadgetry as possible. I've done my best to clarify so anyone can approach the kitchen with confidence. On occasion, I've suggested riffs, leftover uses, and substitutions for the unusual or ways to accommodate allergies. In no time, you'll be grilling lettuces and blitzing romesco like a chef.

Chapters are categorized by menu type as opposed to neighborhood, season, or style. Given the influence of the Pacific Ocean on menus (and psyche), it felt appropriate to grant seafood its own chapter (**Marine Layer**), as well as brunch (**Morning Becomes Eclectic**, so named after the beloved local indie music show). Soups, stews, and grain bowls also deserved their own section (**Hollywood Bowl**). The philosophy behind the pizza recipe, in particular is mixing and matching different recipes as toppings—playing with the culinary crossover that inspired the book, by mashing up recipes found in it.

The variety of a smartly stocked pantry helps encourage better rhythms in the kitchen. If there's uncomplicated deliciousness at your fingertips, delivery becomes far less tantalizing. Californians champion cleaner flavor and less fuss. In bringing the L.A. kitchen into your own, many recipes here can sub in time-saving parts of the whole. For example, if it's overwhelming to candy kumquats for morning granola, simply buy candied tangerines. Ditto for the gelato pie.

Kitchen Notes

- A digital scale is a godsend in the kitchen and worth its, you know, weight.

- So is a fry/candy thermometer.

- Measurements are given in weight when helpful. For baking, weight is given for the sake of the precision involved.

- Butter is unsalted.

- Herbs are fresh unless specified.

- You don't need more than a paring knife, chef's knife, and a serrated bread knife so long as they're sharpened and you know how to slice. For example, for steaks, slice against—perpendicular, not parallel to—the muscle fibers.

- Unless noted otherwise, salt is sea salt. Any quality salt will take you far. Topographic, flaky fleur de sel is generally used for finishing.

- ***Pay close attention when a recipe calls for kosher salt. Here's why:*** Two common brands, Morton kosher salt and Diamond Crystal kosher salt, are substantially different in volume than weight. 1 tablespoon of Morton salt = about 1.85 tablespoons Diamond Crystal kosher salt by weight. I used Diamond Crystal kosher salt but indicated weight and volume in recipes so as to avoid any issues. If you have Morton salt, do not use the Diamond Crystal volume specified in these recipes. Use the weight in grams or your dish will be very salty!

CONSERVE WATER

COCKTAILS AND DRINKS

Kali
Lavender Lemonade

Cofax Coffee
Sticky Honey Chai

The Varnish
Negroni

The Spirit Guild
Orange-Spice Shrub

Eat Your Drink
Stinging Nettle Cocktail

The Walker Inn
P.C.H. Watermelon Soda

The Coconut Club
The Turf

Viviane
Viviane's Pineapple Punch

Gracias Madre
Mezcal Mule

Hinoki & The Bird
The Chandler

Kali / Lavender Lemonade

Plain lemonade is for suckers! This elegant refresher on Kevin Meehan's midsummer menu is redolent of Ojai's rolling purple fields, just outside of L.A. While fragrant lavender overwhelms more subtle flavors, lemon is a worthy partner. Judicious use of culinary lavender—which is additive-free, uses sweeter varietals, and increases in potency as it dries—will steer this cooler away from sachet territory. The method for crafting lavender syrup here can be exchanged with most herbs. Imagine the possibilities: rosemary, lemon verbena, lemon balm, Thai basil, bergamot . . .

MAKES APPROXIMATELY 1 QUART LEMONADE, PLUS ADDITIONAL LAVENDER SYRUP

1 cup sugar

4 cups water

1 heaping tablespoon culinary lavender, roughly chopped

1 cup fresh lemon juice, or to taste

Lavender sprigs, for garnish

Combine the sugar, 1 cup water, and the lavender in a small saucepan and bring to a simmer over medium heat. Once the sugar has dissolved (it'll be tough to see with the flowers, so give it a taste to feel for any sugar crystals on your tongue), turn off the heat and allow the syrup to cool, then strain into a bottle. In the refrigerator, the syrup will keep for up to 1 month.

Pour the lemon juice and the remaining 3 cups water into a pitcher. Add lavender syrup to the desired sweetness, taste, and adjust the acid with more lemon juice as needed. Stir and pour over ice to serve. Garnish glasses with a sprig of fresh lavender.

Cofax Coffee / Sticky Honey Chai

Sticky rice. Sticky yoga mats. Sticky wickets. Not just another example of a peculiar Indian penchant for stickiness, the chai at modern coffee shop Cofax coats a toasty blend of Assam tea and pungent spices with gooey honey and steaming milk. (While we're playing the name game, just as a local wouldn't ask for salsa sauce to go with the Cofax breakfast burrito, don't call it chai tea.) As for ancillary benefits, Nicole Rucker's take packs a boost: digestive black pepper; blood sugar-regulating cinnamon; and anti-inflammatory cardamom, which is also a mood balancer. That said, if you make it dirty and add a shot of espresso, you'll be awake in this (and every) time zone. In PST, head over to the Fairfax District and get yourself a Cofax donut, too.

MAKES 1 CUP CHAI BASE, ENOUGH FOR 4 TO 5 SERVINGS

10 grams cardamom pods, cracked

2½ whole cloves

5 whole black peppercorns, cracked

15 grams cinnamon stick, broken into 1-inch chunks

1 ounce Assam BOP tea

¼ cup honey, plus more as needed

25 grams fresh ginger, juiced (see page 31)

½ cup milk of choice

In a heavy-bottomed pot, toast all the spices over medium-low heat until fragrant, stirring continuously. This is no time to be texting—spices burn quickly! Remove from the heat and transfer the spices to a large bowl to cool. Add the tea and toss to mix.

In a saucepan, heat the honey and ginger juice over low heat to a bare simmer. Remove from the heat and pour the mixture over the bowl of tea and spices, and stir until mixed. Allow to cool completely. Portion into jars, or spoon 3 tablespoons each into individual teabags. Store these in the refrigerator until ready to portion.

To assemble: In a saucepan, bring 3 tablespoons of the sticky chai base and 2 cups water to a simmer over medium-low heat, then turn off the heat. Add the milk and warm over low heat until it is steaming hot but not simmering, so as to avoid boiling the milk. Using a strainer or fine-mesh sieve, separate the solids from the tea. Taste, adjusting the milk and honey as needed, and serve.

For iced chai, chill after straining, and serve over ice.

The Varnish / Negroni

Want to experience the origin of our more recent obsession with Penicillins or Aviations? Check out The Varnish. A partnership between Cedd Moses, Eric Alperin, and Sasha Petraske, the back room behind c.1908 Cole's has captivated creative minds with its resurrection of 1930s speakeasy-era cocktails. For master mixologist Alperin, it's about consistency of technique. Differences are subtle, like identifying the variations in textures and temperatures between, say, shaking and stirring. Negronis are intended to sit on a large block of ice that will slowly melt. As more ice (water) is diluted into the drink, the burn of the alcohol is lessened and more flavor compounds are released. The Varnish intends each "stirred down" cocktail to take a journey: The first sip should be a little bit "hot" and harsh; it should reach its peak as the ice melts; the last sip, a little soft. Enjoy the ride.

MAKES 1

1 ounce Beefeater gin
1 ounce Campari
1 ounce Carpano Antica Formula vermouth
Orange twist

Using a jigger, measure the ingredients into a 9-ounce rocks glass. Add a large block of cold ice and stir twice. Express an orange twist over the glass and serve immediately.

MASTERING THE NEGRONI:

- The Varnish's classic Negroni uses a 1:1:1 ratio for balanced flavor, texture, and alcohol-by-volume (ABV). Adjust this ratio to suit your palate and to your ingredients: Is your gin 80 proof or 94? Do you prefer a richer vermouth? Whatever your preference, perfect your pour so you can easily recreate that ratio every time.

- The right ratio demands an accurate pour, so calibrate that jigger! Get out a digital scale and make sure a 1-ounce pour weighs 29.6 grams. There should be a straight "wash line" instead of a curved meniscus.

- It is critical to use one large block of frosty (not sweaty) ice straight out of the freezer per drink. Negronis and other "stirred down" cocktails change in flavor, texture, and ABV as the ice melts. Using a single, large block of very cold ice slows this journey and extends the sweet spot between first and last sips. No large blocks? Fill your glass with as much frosty ice as you can.

- To finish: Peel a substantial twist from a fresh orange with a firm peel. To express its essential oils, hold the twist in your fingers about two inches above and an inch *behind* the glass, and squeeze. Alperin points out that bitter molecules are larger, and will drop straight down, while the more aromatic compounds are lighter and will float before raining into the cocktail, resulting in a less harsh flavor.

The Spirit Guild / Orange-Spice Shrub

Capturing the essences of California, The Spirit Guild's Miller Duvall, Max Parry, and Morgan McLachlan use clementine oranges harvested from Duvall's family orchards near Bakersfield for their small-batch vodka and gin. The Spirit Guild also draws inspiration from tiki culture, one of great innovations of Los Angeles (thanks, Don the Beachcomber!). Cinnamon and clove are common spice notes in tiki drinks, as is almond via orgeat and falernum. This tiki-inspired shrub and cocktail from the DTLA distillery/tasting room trades almond in for fruitier pistachio, both because it's local and it's one of the botanicals used in TSG's Astral Pacific Gin.

Aromatic shrubs and fizzy water are super refreshing with or without booze. They're also an un-fussy cocktail for hosts: Steep and strain the shrub ahead of time, and mix together the spirits and soda with ice when friends arrive.

MAKES 1¾ CUPS SHRUB, ENOUGH FOR ABOUT 20 COCKTAILS

1 orange, peeled and cut into ½-inch cubes

1 cup sugar

4 cinnamon sticks

⅓ cup roasted shelled pistachios, lightly crushed

6 whole cloves

1 cup distilled white vinegar

FOR EACH COCKTAIL:

1½ ounces gin

1 ounce shrub

Soda Water

To prepare the shrub: In a 1-quart jar, combine the chopped orange, sugar, cinnamon, pistachios, and cloves. Cover and briefly dry shake to combine. Refrigerate for at least 24 hours.

The next day, add the vinegar and shake until the sugar begins to dissolve, and let sit for another 24 hours. Filter through cheesecloth or a nut-milk bag into a clean jar or bottle. If not using immediately, refrigerate until ready to use (tightly sealed, the shrub can keep up to 6 weeks).

To assemble a shrub cocktail: For each cocktail, fill a double old-fashioned glass with cracked ice. Add 1½ ounces gin and 1 ounce of the shrub, and top with soda water. Gently stir clockwise six times and serve.

Eat Your Drink / Stinging Nettle Cocktail

When Matthew Biancaniello first popped up at the Hollywood Roosevelt hotel, he wasn't mixing just any old martini. Each cocktail was a doctor's orders sort of affair, and his fascination with unusual tinctures and tonics helped introduce L.A. to a more alchemical approach to mixology. Well versed in foraging and beekeeping, and a familiar face at the Santa Monica Farmers' Market, Biancaniello continues to blur the lines of culinary and cocktailing with his wild creations.

Young spring nettles are prized for their subtle nutty notes. The bright leaves cook down into creamed soups, sauté well with garlic and pine nuts, and they top a mean green pizza. Here is one of those ingredients you can literally only touch for a brief moment in the cool beauty of early spring. Formic acid is what accounts for that nasty sting, so wear thick gloves when handling them (and long pants, should you decide to go foraging in a thicket).

MAKES ½ BOTTLE INFUSED VODKA, ENOUGH FOR ABOUT 5 COCKTAILS

½ pound fresh young stinging nettles

350-ml (half of a standard 750-ml bottle) vodka, for infusing

2 whole cloves

1 ounce (2 tablespoons) blood orange juice

¾ ounce (1⅓ tablespoons) fresh lime juice

¾ ounce (1 tablespoon) agave syrup

Sparkling red wine, such as lambrusco, for topping

FOR EACH COCKTAIL:

2 ounces infused vodka

1 ounce blood orange juice

To infuse the vodka: Wearing gloves, place the nettles in an airtight jar, and top with the vodka, making sure they are submerged. Cover and set aside to infuse out of direct sun for 1 week, shaking the jar daily.

Using a strainer or cheesecloth, strain the vodka into a measuring cup and discard the nettles. Either clean the jar and transfer the vodka back, or transfer to a hermetically sealed bottle. Chill until ready to use.

The night or morning before you plan to mix the cocktail, put the cloves in the blood orange juice. Set aside to infuse.

To mix the cocktail: In a shaker filled with ice, combine 2 ounces infused vodka, 1 ounce blood orange juice, the lime juice, and agave syrup. Cover, shake, and double-strain into a glass without ice. Top with sparkling red wine.

The Walker Inn / P.C.H. Watermelon Soda

In an impressive flourish of technique-driven high gastronomy, *omakase*-style cocktail bar The Walker Inn, at the rear of the Hotel Normandie, captivates like none other. Once a drink menu has been revealed, it's never repeated. Highlighting the sunny friendship between sherry and melon, this beach cooler by Alex Day and Devon Tarby was on the opening progression dedicated to the Pacific Coast Highway. A watermelon-y trip up the 101, this carbonated intermezzo is paired with picnic-ready "beach popcorn" coated with liquefied coconut oil and Himalayan sea salt. Palm trees, optional.

MAKES 3

3 chunks watermelon, rind and seeds removed

1 ounce gin

¾ ounce Aperol

¾ ounce fresh lemon juice

¾ ounce simple syrup

¼ ounce La Gitana Manzanilla Sherry

2 ounces seltzer water

Watermelon wedges, for garnish

Cayenne, for garnish

Sea salt, for garnish

In a cocktail shaker, muddle the watermelon. Add the gin, Aperol, lemon juice, simple syrup, and sherry, cover, and shake. Double strain into a carbonating bottle. Carbonate and chill. Re-carbonate before serving. Add up to 2 ounces seltzer, to taste.

Pour the drinks into stemless wineglasses and garnish with a watermelon triangle on top. Dust with cayenne and a few flakes of sea salt.

The Coconut Club / The Turf

There's something deliciously subversive about turning a health-craze staple like green juice (here, a fine-tuned blend of pineapple, kiwi, apple, spinach, and shishito pepper) into a heady, herby cocktail. Mixology mastermind Nathan Hazard and chef Andy Windak upend expectations at their residency-style Coconut Club, proffering cocktail progressions that move through moods and narratives with inventive accompaniments, garnishes, and serving styles.

For the Turf, consider following Hazard and Windauk's directions for a truly over-the-top garnish: Cut a flatiron steak into thick slices, rub each with ground coffee, salt, and pepper, and sear on each side in a cast-iron pan. Toss whole shishito peppers with olive oil and blister in the same hot pan till just blackened, then serve each drink with a skewer of seared coffee-rubbed steak and a blistered pepper.

MAKES 4

GREEN JUICE
2 cups fresh pineapple chunks
1 kiwi, peeled
1 large Granny Smith apple, cored
Handful of spinach
1 shishito pepper

GREEN TEA SYRUP
1 cup water
1 tablespoon loose-leaf green tea
1 cup sugar

TO ASSEMBLE
8 ounces blanco tequila
4 ounces green Chartreuse
4 ounces fresh lime juice
4 Thai basil sprigs, for garnish

To make the juice: Juice the fruit and vegetables in the order listed, according to the machine's instructions. Strain through a fine-mesh sieve and use immediately or refrigerate for up to 2 days.

To make the green tea syrup: In a saucepan, bring the water to a boil. Add the tea leaves, remove from the heat, then cover and set aside to infuse for 5 minutes. Strain the tea and return it to the saucepan over medium heat, discarding the leaves. Add the sugar and cook, stirring, until the sugar has completely dissolved. Take off the heat and allow the syrup to cool. (In a glass container in the refrigerator, the syrup will keep for up to 1 month.)

To assemble: For each cocktail, in a cocktail shaker, combine 2 ounces of the green juice, ⅔ ounce of the green tea syrup, 2 ounces of the tequila, 1 ounce of the Chartreuse, and 1 ounce of the lime juice. Add ice, cover, and shake. Strain into a large double old-fashioned glass filled with cracked ice. Garnish with a fan-like sprig of Thai basil (with optional skewered steak and shishito pepper).

Viviane / Viviane's Pineapple Punch

A sip of this midcentury-inspired rum punch for escapists will transport you: maybe to the ring-a-ding swing of parties up in the Hollywood Hills; to Trader Vic's and Don the Beachcomber; or to 2018, and a chic poolside cabana at the Avalon Hotel in Beverly Hills.

Indeed, you can't make a true Mai Tai or tiki drink like this one without orgeat. What's this staple of throwback cocktailing? In the nineteenth century, the French made a floral barley water, and over time, they swapped out the grain in favor of sweet almonds and orange blossom. Hit up a quality liquor store for a bottle, or you can make your own like Viviane bartender Ryan Wainwright.

MAKES 1

1½ ounces Hamilton Guyana Rum
½ ounce aromatic bitters
¾ ounce lime juice
¾ ounce pineapple juice
¾ ounce orgeat
Pineapple wedge, for garnish
Cherry, for garnish

Fill a shaker half full (or half empty, depending on your world view) with ice. Add the ingredients (except the garnishes) and shake hard and fast, until very cold. Double strain into a tall double old-fashioned glass over 1 large ice cube. Garnish with the pineapple wedge and cherry.

Gracias Madre / Mezcal Mule

Even before its more recent surge in popularity, the Moscow Mule has been a Los Angeles institution as far as cocktails are concerned. Jack Morgan of the now closed Cock 'n Bull Restaurant on Sunset Boulevard (and Cock 'n Bull ginger beer) created it in the 1940s with an alcohol distributor on the East Coast. The unmistakable copper cup was a promotional tool given to bartenders as proof of its popularity.

Jason Eisner's tequila cocktails have the design-chic bar patrons at plant-centric Gracias Madre standing three deep. As cooler nights set in wherever you are, crank the outdoor heaters and kick two feet up on the deck table for your own Gracias Madre happy hour. Here's Eisner's smoky twist on the classic Moscow Mule, which ditches the vodka for mezcal and makes a ginger beer in the shaker. Key to this is the dry shake to keep the cocktail light and frothy. If you need ginger juice, simply blend fresh ginger with a little lime juice and water, then strain though cheesecloth.

MAKES 1

2 ounces mezcal
½ ounce fresh lime juice
½ ounce ginger juice
1 ounce raw agave nectar
1½ ounces sparkling water

TO ASSEMBLE
1 sprig mint (optional)
Lime quarter (optional)

Combine all the ingredients in a cocktail shaker and dry shake for 10 seconds. Be careful, as the bubbles in the sparkling water will give a little pushback. Strain into a copper Mule mug. Add fresh rocks to the top of the glass.

Garnish with a sprig of mint and a quartered lime, if you'd like.

Hinoki & The Bird / The Chandler

Keeping in line with the ethos of craft cocktailing, mixologist Gregory Wescott makes his own vanilla bean-orange syrup to soften this cherry-vanilla dream fortified with plenty of Buffalo Trace bourbon. Local industry favorite Miracle Mile Sour Cherry Bitters also comes to play in this cocktail.

Muddling is only necessary when you have ingredients that don't break up easily—like fruit or leafy herbs. Still, there can be too much of a good thing. Overmuddling citrus leads to tartness; herbs, bitterness.

MAKES 1

2 Bing cherries, pitted, plus ½ cherry for garnish

2 ounces bourbon

¾ ounce vanilla or orange-vanilla syrup

Juice of ¾ lemon

2 dashes of Miracle Mile Sour Cherry Bitters

Ground cardamom, for garnish

Put the cherries in a shaker and smash them with a muddler. Add the bourbon, vanilla syrup, lemon juice, and bitters. Fill with ice, cover, and shake vigorously for 12 seconds.

Pour into a rocks glass over cubed ice. Garnish with the cherry half and a light sprinkle of cardamom.

DIVE IN
SMALL PLATES AND STARTERS

Farmshop
Avocado Hummus with Pistachio Salsa Verde

The Bazaar by José Andrés
Jicama-Wrapped Guacamole with Chipotle Salsa

Local Kitchen + Wine Bar
Grilled Speck-Wrapped Persimmon

Madcapra
White Bean Spread with Black Olives and Marjoram

Alimento
Bagna Cauda

Norah
Cauliflower "Popcorn" with Chickpea Tahini and Fermented Chile Sauce

Pine & Crane
Beef Roll

Salazar
Esquites (Mexican Street Corn)

Adana
Dolmeh (Stuffed Grape Leaves)

Otium
Baja Yellowtail Tostada with Peach-Habañero Salsa and Avocado Puree

Angelini Osteria
Fig & Gorgonzola Gratin

Moon Juice
Cultured Nut Cheese

Café Gratitude
Garlic Tahini Sauce

Manhattan Beach Post
Red Chimichurri

Homage to the Avocado Toast

Farmshop / Avocado Hummus with Pistachio Salsa Verde

At the time of Farmshop's 2010 opening at the Brentwood Country Mart, Jeffrey Cerciello's paean to California's distinct style of clean, modern farmhouse cooking was a pioneering move—and one designed by Commune, too. The career veteran of The French Laundry was spot-on to bet that the philosophies and localism of NorCal's wine country would be received, and understood, in the SoCal sunshine.

Neither guacamole nor truly hummus, with its seedy pistachio salsa and whipped avocado, this velvety hummus takes advantage of the former's crunch and the latter's texture. It's a marvel of earthiness that lacks the heaviness you get with most bean dips. It's also great with a glass of rosé.

MAKES ABOUT 4 CUPS

AVOCADO HUMMUS
4 garlic cloves
½ cup canola oil
2 tablespoons Dijon mustard
Juice of 2 lemons
Salt
2 cups drained cooked (or canned) chickpeas
5 tablespoons tahini
½ cup ice
1 cup olive oil
3 ripe avocados

PISTACHIO SALSA VERDE
⅔ cup shelled raw pistachios
Zest of 3 lemons
Juice of 1 lemon
3½ tablespoons thinly sliced chives
2½ tablespoons chopped parsley
3½ tablespoons extra-virgin olive oil
Salt

Nigella seeds or black sesame seeds, for garnish (optional)
Flatbread or crackers, for serving

To make the hummus: In a small pot, combine the garlic and canola oil. Simmer gently over medium heat until tender, about 10 minutes. Transfer to a food processor and add the mustard and half the lemon juice. Season with salt and pulse until smooth. Scrape down the sides of the bowl with a spatula and add the chickpeas. With the machine running, slowly drizzle in the tahini, then add the ice and ½ cup of the olive oil, scraping down the bowl when necessary. Season with salt, then transfer the hummus to a bowl and set aside.

Without cleaning out the processor, halve, seed, and scoop the avocado flesh directly into the machine with the remaining lemon juice. Puree, slowly streaming in the remaining ½ cup olive oil. Stop the processor and scrape down the sides. Season with salt and gently fold into the chickpea puree.

To make the pistachio salsa: Preheat the oven to 350°F. Spread the pistachios in an even layer on a rimmed baking sheet and toast for 3 to 5 minutes, until fragrant and lightly browned. Give them a shake every minute or so, as pistachios can burn quickly. Transfer to a cutting board and coarsely chop while warm. Combine the still-warm pistachios in a bowl with the lemon zest, lemon juice, chives, parsley, and olive oil; season with salt.

To assemble: Top the avocado hummus with spoonfuls of the pistachio salsa, a drizzle of oil, and a sprinkle of salt and nigella or black sesame seeds, if using. Farmshop serves za'atar-seasoned lavash crackers alongside, but any savory flatbread or rustic cracker will pair nicely.

The Bazaar by José Andrés / Jicama-Wrapped Guacamole with Chipotle Salsa

Superstar chef José Andrés created a Jim Henson-like fantasy–albeit for high gastronomy–in giving Los Angeles The Bazaar. A star on the menu: these morralitos (little purses), which were once served as small bites at Andrés's pioneering Café Atlantico in D.C. in the mid-1990s. At that time, beggar's purses were "it dish" material; those who dined well in the 1980s or 1990s likely came across that bite of filled crêpe, tied with chive, much imitated but born at New York's Quilted Giraffe. Intrigued by the idea of unconventional ravioli, Andrés plays with fillings like guacamole and smoky salsa. In lieu of crêpe, he slices cool, juicy jicama sashimi-thin as his wrapper. The "wait, I know that taste–what is that?" surprise is crushed Fritos for the win.

MAKES 12 TO 16

GUACAMOLE
¼ cup minced red onion

1 serrano chile, seeded

5 tablespoons minced cilantro

6 tablespoons fresh lime juice (from about 3 limes), or to taste

1 tablespoon extra-virgin olive oil

7 ripe avocados, peeled, pitted and lightly mashed

3 tablespoons (1 ounce) Diamond Crystal kosher salt

CHIPOTLE SALSA
8 dried 2-inch chipotle chiles (about 1½ ounces)

½ teaspoon cumin seeds

8 whole Roma (plum) tomatoes

2 tablespoons cilantro leaves

1 tablespoon minced or pureed garlic

Pinch of salt, plus more as needed

½ cup thinly sliced Spanish onion

TO ASSEMBLE
1 whole jicama, peeled and shaved/sliced extremely thin

Fritos corn chips, crushed

Very finely diced tomato

5 micro cilantro sprigs (optional)

To make the guacamole: In a molcajete or food processor, grind the onion, chile, and cilantro, then add small amounts of the lime juice and olive oil at a time. Once fully incorporated, scoop in the avocado flesh and gently stir. Add the salt and check for seasoning; add more lime juice if needed. Set aside.

To make the chipotle salsa: Rehydrate the chipotles in warm water for 20 minutes, or until softened.

Heat a cast-iron pan over medium-high heat. Once hot but not smoking, toast the cumin seeds, stirring frequently to avoid burning. Immediately smash the toasted seeds with the back of your knife, or pound in a molcajete, and set aside.

On a stovetop burner or grill, char the outside of the tomatoes until the peels are blackened. Peel the tomatoes and place in a blender. Add the chipotle, cilantro, garlic, cumin, and salt. Puree until smooth. Taste and season as needed; stir in the onion and transfer to a small serving bowl.

To assemble: Spread the jicama sheets on a serving platter. Crush 1 teaspoon worth of corn chips in the center of each slice. Spoon the guacamole on top, then sprinkle each with 1 teaspoon diced tomato. Close the jicama by making a variant of a beggar's purse, gathering the jicama around the filling and pulling all sides up and in toward the center. Or, simply fold them like a taco. (You may need a toothpick or chive tie to keep them closed in either case.) Garnish with micro cilantro, if desired, and serve with the chipotle salsa on the side.

Local Kitchen + Wine Bar / Grilled Speck-Wrapped Persimmon

Think elegance in flip-flops, and you'll understand the ethos behind Santa Monica's Local Kitchen. Much like the age-old combinations of melon and prosciutto, or dates and bacon, this sweet-savory breezy canapé plays Southern California's beloved fall persimmon off applewood-smoked speck hot and crisp from the grill. It's like the charcuterie board gone rogue.

Source Fuyu, not Hachiya, persimmons for this recipe. These are the flatter, wider varietal that can be eaten raw like apples. As a finger food for parties, instead of toothpicks, try a sprig of rosemary or lavender, with just enough of the herbs removed. It looks pretty and smells divine.

MAKES 24 TO 32

4 medium-large Fuyu persimmons

La Quercia Speck Americano, (6 to 10 slices)

Aged balsamic vinegar, for drizzling

6 to 8 large basil leaves, for garnish

Heat a grill to medium. On a clean cutting surface, using a paring knife, peel and core the persimmon, then slice into 6 to 8 wedges. Cut the speck into 2- to 3-inch-long strips that are the same height as the persimmon wedges. Wrap each wedge tightly. Place the wrapped wedges on the grill and cook until the speck is charred and slightly crisp, but not blackened, and the fruit is hot and tender. Using tongs or a spatula, transfer to a platter.

While still warm, drizzle with balsamic vinegar. Tear the basil and scatter over the top. Serve immediately.

Madcapra / White Bean Spread with Black Olives and Marjoram

With its pungent marjoram and chopped olive topping, this lush spread from Sara Kramer and Sarah Hymanson of Madcapra and Kismet is a filling appetizer that's handy to have around when guests arrive toting a bottle of wine. You don't need much more than to serve it with warmed lavash as a dipping vehicle. A quick word on beans and dry goods: Cannellini, great northern, and, strangely enough, navy beans are all "white beans," differentiated mostly by size. Any will work.

SERVES 6

3 cups (250 grams) uncooked white beans

3 tablespoons (40 grams) extra-virgin olive oil

3 garlic cloves, unpeeled

1 onion, halved

½ lemon

½ cinnamon stick

1 bay leaf (fresh, if possible)

2⅓ cups water

Salt

½ cup (150 grams) tahini

1 small-medium garlic clove

4 teaspoons fresh lemon juice, plus more as needed

1 cup Moroccan oil-cured olives, pitted and chopped

2 tablespoons sesame seeds, toasted

3 tablespoons fresh marjoram leaves

Extra-virgin olive oil, for garnish

Put the beans in a large bowl and add 9 cups water. Set aside to soak overnight. The next morning, drain and rinse.

In a large pot, heat the olive oil over medium heat until shimmering. Smash but don't bother to peel 2 of the garlic cloves, and add them to the pot with the onions and the lemon half, cut-side down. Brown the garlic and onions, stirring frequently, to avoid burning.

Add the cinnamon stick and bay leaf, followed by the soaked beans and 2 cups of the water. Increase the heat to high and bring the water to a boil, then reduce the heat and simmer the beans until very creamy but not burst, about 1 hour. (Not all the water will have been absorbed.) Season with salt. Turn off the heat and allow the beans to cool in their cooking liquid.

While the beans cook, combine the tahini, the remaining garlic clove (peeled), remaining ⅓ cup water, ¾ teaspoon salt, and the lemon juice in a food processor. Process until smooth and thick. Transfer to a container to chill until the beans are cooled.

Drain the cooled beans and transfer to the food processor, discarding the cooking liquid. Puree the beans, then return the tahini mixture to the processor and continue processing until very smooth. Taste and adjust the seasoning with salt and lemon juice.

Transfer the dip to a serving bowl. Top with the olives, sesame seeds, marjoram, and a generous slosh of olive oil. Serve chilled or at room temperature.

Alimento / Bagna Cauda

Portioned in small fondue pots or terra-cotta bowls, the garlicky spring "fondue" of rustic Piedmontese cooking has dipped its way into L.A. menus in recent years. At Alimento in Silverlake, it's served quite traditionally with vegetables and a late swirl-in of sous-vide 62-degree egg. (Optionally, to mimic this, add in a poached egg, as indicated at the end of the recipe.) The hot bath of velvety, salty, market-driven umami is worth the effort of peeling the garlic. It is an *enormous* amount. Don't skip the garlic's first bath in milk; this poaching is essential to soothe its pungency.

SERVES 4 TO 6

6¼ cups garlic cloves (about 100 cloves or 6 heads)

4 cups milk

2 (50-gram) tins salt-packed anchovies, cleaned and soaked in water for 1 hour

½ cup olive oil

½ cup (1 stick) butter, in 1-tablespoon pieces

Raw, steamed, or roasted vegetables, for dipping

Country bread, torn into chunks, for dipping

1 poached egg, kept warm (see page 115)

Combine the garlic and milk in a medium saucepan over medium heat. As soon as the milk begins to boil, turn off the heat. Drain the garlic, discarding the milk.

Rinse the garlic and return it to the pot. Add the anchovies and ¼ cup of the olive oil, and stir over very low heat. Cook for 1 hour, or until the anchovies have dissolved and the garlic is extremely soft. Using a potato masher or firm whisk, crush the garlic in the pot until you achieve a porridge-like consistency. Stir in the remaining ¼ cup olive oil and the butter, till melted.

Serve warm, with any assortment of raw, steamed, or roasted vegetables and chunks of country bread. Once half the dip is eaten, add the poached egg to finish.

Norah / Cauliflower "Popcorn" with Chickpea Tahini and Fermented Chile Sauce

With slabs of marble, taupe leathers, and natural materials and textures, Norah slid into the WeHo dining scene and quickly joined the essential patios club dominated by Eveleigh, Sunset Tower, and Chateau Marmont. With these cauliflower poppers, it's a delight to translate that al fresco experience at home. Especially as summer approaches, Fresno chiles (red jalapeños) are plentiful and inexpensive. You can replace them with green jalapeños or another red chile. Spice-reticent cooks can tame the heat by removing seeds and cutting in red bell pepper.

SERVES 4 TO 6

FERMENTED CHILE SAUCE

2 pounds Fresno chiles, stems and half of the seeds removed

2 garlic cloves

1½ tablespoons salt

CHICKPEA TAHINI

3 cups drained cooked (or canned) chickpeas

2 teaspoons smoked paprika

½ teaspoon cayenne

½ cup tahini

1 teaspoon minced garlic

Salt

Fresh lemon juice

CAULIFLOWER "POPCORN"

2 cups rice bran oil or other high-smoke-point oil

3 cups rice flour

1 cup cornstarch

1 tablespoon baking powder

3 tablespoons salt

2 tablespoons ground turmeric

1 tablespoon garlic powder

1 tablespoon onion powder

1 teaspoon cayenne

1 teaspoon smoked paprika

1 large head cauliflower, cut into bite-size florets

To make the fermented chile sauce: In a food processor, combine the chiles, garlic, and salt and process to a paste. Transfer to a very clean, very dry glass jar. Cover with a tightly woven cloth and secure with a rubber band. Leave in a cool, dry place for 3 to 5 days, until a slightly tart flavor has developed. (Depending on how cool/warm your kitchen is, this might take up to a week.) As the chile sauce ferments, the pulp will separate from the liquid, so dutifully stir at least twice daily to release carbon dioxide from the jar and keep the pulp submerged in the liquid. Once the sauce has successfully fermented and begins to taste a little sour and spicy, refrigerate in an airtight container. (The sauce will keep for up to 1 month.)

To make the chickpea tahini: In a blender, combine the chickpeas, paprika, cayenne, tahini, garlic, salt to taste, and a squeeze of lemon juice, and puree. With the machine running, add enough water so the puree reaches a smooth thickness for dipping. Taste and season with salt and lemon juice. Set aside in a bowl.

To make the cauliflower "popcorn": In a large cast-iron skillet (or Dutch oven), heat the rice bran oil to 350°F. Place a wire rack over a baking sheet lined with paper towels.

In a large bowl, combine the rice flour, cornstarch, baking powder, salt, turmeric, garlic powder, onion powder, cayenne, and paprika. In a steady stream, add cold water, stirring until you reach a thin pancake batter consistency.

Working quickly, dredge each floret in the batter and carefully drop them in the hot oil. Fry in batches, a few at a time, until a pale golden brown a shade or two darker than a french fry. Remove each batch from the oil using a basket, skimmer, or tongs, and drain on the prepared rack. Season with salt and repeat with the remaining cauliflower. Serve hot, with the tahini and fermented chile sauce alongside.

Pine & Crane / Beef Roll

Consensus is that the beef roll is a distinctly Sino-Angeleno phenomenon. A spin on tradition unseen beyond L.A. city limits, this version, offered at packed Silverlake hotspot Pine & Crane, irresistibly marries beef braised slow-and-low in rich aromatics with cooling cucumber, green onion, and cilantro. It's reminiscent of Taiwanese and Northern Chinese *shaobing*, a beef-onion handheld bread, and the *niu rou jianbing*, a crêpe-like green onion pancake rolled with beef and sweet bean paste.

The thin Chinese pancakes for wrapping Peking Duck are the home stand-in for the delicious griddled ones Vivian Ku crafts at the restaurant. They're most often found in the frozen aisle and need only to be steamed or reheated before assembly.

MAKES ABOUT 6 FULL-SIZE ROLLS

2 beef shanks, trimmed (1½ to 2 pounds)

2 teaspoons plus 1 tablespoon canola oil, plus more as needed

4 to 6 slices fresh ginger

6 dried chiles de árbol

½ bunch green onions

½ chunk rock sugar

½ teaspoon ground white pepper

6 to 8 star anise pods

1 small cinnamon stick

2 pieces Chinese licorice (see Note)

3 cardamom pods

1 teaspoon ground fennel

1 teaspoon ground cloves

1 teaspoon Sichuan peppercorns

1 cup rice wine

3½ cups soy sauce

TO ASSEMBLE

1 cup hoisin sauce

Chinese pancakes, thawed

2 cucumbers, julienned

½ cup cilantro leaves, coarsely chopped

2 green onions, sliced

Put the beef shank in a large stockpot and add water to cover. Bring to a boil over medium heat and cook for 30 minutes. Remove the shank, discard the water, and set aside.

In a large Dutch oven, heat 2 teaspoons of the canola oil over medium heat. Add the ginger, chiles de árbol, and ½ bunch green onions and cook, stirring, until fragrant, about 4 minutes. Add the rock sugar, white pepper, star anise, cinnamon, Chinese licorice, cardamom, fennel, cloves, Sichuan peppercorns, rice wine, and soy sauce. Put the beef in the pot and add enough water to submerge. Braise over low heat for 2 hours, or until fork-tender. Without draining the liquid, remove the meat from the pot and set it on a cutting board. Slice or shred and set aside. (Your dog will thank you for the bone.)

Pass the leftover braising liquid through a strainer into a bowl. In a separate small bowl, begin stirring the straining liquid into the hoisin sauce until a smooth paste forms, up to 1 cup, and discard the rest. Set aside.

Steam or reheat the thawed Chinese pancakes in a hot skillet until pliable and spotty golden brown.

To assemble the rolls: Brush 1 tablespoon of the sauce evenly across the surface of each pancake. Layer slices of beef, followed by cucumber, cilantro, and green onions. Starting from the bottom, slowly roll the wrap away from you, keeping it tight. Slice and serve immediately.

Note: While there's not much in this recipe, Chinese licorice can affect certain medications like corticosteroids, diuretics, hormones, and blood pressure medication. Let your guests know, or when in doubt, leave it out.

Salazar / Esquites (Mexican Street Corn)

At Salazar, Edras Ochoa and Aaron Melendrez's mostly al fresco patio in Frogtown, this clever take on L.A.'s favorite street food—a freshly roasted ear of corn slathered in mayo, cotija cheese, and Tajín—is served stylishly off the cob as a creamy, smoky, lightly spiced dip. To avoid a gloppy consistency, use European-style as opposed to Greek-style yogurt. Check Latin American markets or farmers' markets for pungent fresh epazote, which doesn't have a great stand-in; you might see it labeled as wormseed, Mexican tea, Jesuit's tea, herba sancti mariae, or paico.

Do you know Tajín? Just as a Mexican flag is red, white, and green, Tajín blends chile powder, salt, and dehydrated lime in one delicious, ubiquitous condiment. A big bottle or handy travel-size shaker is a common sight. Equally at home rimming a michelada, sprinkled liberally on a fruity *paleta* (see page 212), or here, Tajín is to Angelenos what Old Bay is to most Marylanders.

SERVES 4 TO 6

1 to 2 Fresno chiles

8 ears fresh white corn, shucked

6 ounces aioli or mayonnaise

4 ounces cotija cheese, grated

1 tablespoon sea salt, divided

2 tablespoons chopped fresh epazote

½ cup plain yogurt

¼ to ½ cup mascarpone cheese (or crema, yogurt, sour cream, or crème fraîche)

1 teaspoon garlic powder

Tajín powder (or chile powder), for garnish

Stem and slice the Fresno peppers into thin rings or cubes, and set aside. (Remove the seeds if you are sensitive to heat.)

Heat a grill. Place the corn on the grates and char until evenly blackened, about 25 minutes, turning the corn every 3 to 5 minutes. (If using a broiler, paint the corn with olive oil and place on a broiler pan under the broiler, rotating every 5 minutes for 20 minutes total.) Using tongs, transfer to a clean cutting surface and let cool enough to handle. Using a sharp knife, shave off the kernels, and transfer to a large bowl. Add the aioli, cotija cheese, ½ tablespoon salt, and half the epazote. Mix thoroughly until well incorporated.

In a small bowl, mix together the yogurt, mascarpone, the remaining ½ tablespoon sea salt (or to taste), and the garlic powder until you reach a creamy consistency. Add the mixture into the corn in small increments and mix well until the consistency is creamy but not gloppy—add according to taste; you may not need all of it. Transfer to a serving bowl and dust with the Tajín. Garnish with the Fresno chiles and the remaining epazote.

Adana / Dolmeh (Stuffed Grape Leaves)

Dolma, dolmeh, dolmades. These humble, palm-of-your-hand packages of stuffed vegetable–here, grape leaves–are like beloved characters in sitcom crossovers, appearing in cuisines the way one character might be found in two Thursday night shows. Here in Glendale at Adana, the crossover is Persian-Armenian with a little L.A. Edward Khechemya, beloved second-generation restaurateur, says it's "85% Persian, 15% mine."

In this party-size recipe, a tomato base bound with Turkish pepper paste infuses rice with sun-dried intensity. Lemon juice, parsley, and dill cool a small mountain of spices including Aleppo pepper and cumin. Roll the herb-flecked starch into California grape leaves, and don't be shy about adding the olive oil and lemon juice. When served cold with lemons and garlicky tzatziki, the flavors of dolmeh shine, especially after a day or two. Bonus: A scoop of the uber-sticky, tart rice filling complements lighter preparations like grilled or steamed fish.

MAKES ABOUT 100 DOLMEH

2 cups vegetable oil

2 yellow onions, chopped

2 tablespoons tomato paste

1 tablespoon hot red pepper paste

1 tablespoon sweet red pepper paste

5½ cups water

4 cups Chinese sticky rice (short-grain)

2 bunches green onions, chopped

1 bunch dill, chopped

2 bunches flat-leaf parsley, chopped

10 garlic cloves, minced

1¼ to 1½ cups lemon juice

1 jalapeño, seeded and finely chopped

1½ teaspoons freshly ground black pepper

1 tablespoon ground Aleppo pepper

½ teaspoon ground cumin

1½ tablespoons salt

Jarred grape leaves, rinsed, for rolling

Lemon wedges, for serving

In a large saucepan, warm 1½ cups of the vegetable oil over medium heat until just shimmering. Add the onions and reduce the heat slightly. Cook, stirring continuously, so they sweat but don't sizzle or brown, 10 to 12 minutes.

Add the tomato and red pepper pastes, one at a time, incorporating each before adding the next. Pour in 4½ cups of the water and stir until combined. Cover and cook until the mixture is just bubbling on its sides. You want to keep the tomato from drying out, so keep a close eye.

Wash and add the rice, stir, then add the remaining 1 cup water. Bring the mixture to a simmer and cook for about 10 minutes, until al dente. Add the green onions, dill, parsley, and garlic–stirring everything in will take a minute (and a little muscle–the mixture will be thick).

Transfer the spiced rice to a large bowl. Pour in ¾ to 1 cup of the lemon juice and mix thoroughly. Add the jalapeño, black pepper, Aleppo pepper, cumin, and salt and mix to fully combine. Check the seasoning, adding more lemon juice if necessary. Cover and refrigerate overnight.

The next day, cover the bottom of a large stockpot with grape leaves. Flip a saucer upside down and place it in the bottom of the pot.

On a clean, flat surface, layer 2 leaves on top of each other, staggered, so that the tip of one leaf is at the bottom of the next. Into the center, spoon 2 tablespoons of the rice and shape it into a crosswise mound about 2 inches long. Like rolling a burrito, pull the left and right sides up and over the mixture, and holding

CONTINUED

them steady, pull the bottom of the grape leaves up and over the center. Keeping the shape intact, roll the dolmeh away from you to close. When complete, place each in the pot, piling them around the saucer.

When all are in the pot, place another saucer, upside down, on top to hold down the dolmeh. Add the remaining ½ cup lemon juice, ½ cup vegetable oil, and just enough water to almost cover the dolmeh, without submerging the top saucer. Cover and bring to a boil over medium-high heat. Cook for 10 minutes. (Avoid oversteaming, or the dolmeh will fall apart.)

Gently remove the steamed dolmeh from the pot with tongs and transfer to a platter to cool, reserving the liquid. Serve with lemon wedges once cooled or chill, covered. Leftover dolmeh can be kept in an airtight container in the boiling liquid for up to 1 week.

Otium / Baja Yellowtail Tostada with Peach-Habañero Salsa and Avocado Puree

Next to The Broad museum is a marvelous setting for chef Tim Hollingsworth to create works of edible beauty. Take this tostada, for example. From afar, the confetti of ingredients could pass for a painting of abstract expressionism! It features brined and quick-seared Baja yellowtail with tiny tomatoes, peaches, cilantro blossoms, micro mint, and shaved radish all splashed with lime juice. A silky avocado puree refreshes like a smoothie with kick; the hot peach salsa could double as a killer chilled soup or liven up simple grilled meats.

Hollingsworth makes his own crisp, flagstone-sized tortillas that float to the table. You can purchase your own or use soft corn or flour tortillas and simply bake them in a hot oven until crisp and the edges start to curl. Poolside or served with salt-rimmed margaritas or cold beer, baked or fried, you can see why tostadas are one of L.A.'s beloved seafood standbys.

SERVES 4

YELLOWTAIL AND BRINE
1 cup (140 grams) Diamond Crystal kosher salt

Zest of 3 oranges

Zest of 4 limes

5 bay leaves (fresh, if possible)

10 cups water

2 pounds Baja yellowtail

Salt and freshly ground black pepper

PEACH-HABAÑERO SALSA
Canola oil

3 cups julienned white onions (about 2 medium)

1 to 2 habañero chiles, stemmed

1 pound whole firm peaches, pitted, peeled, and halved

10 to 13 (10 grams) chiles de árbol

2 (1-inch) slices peeled fresh ginger

½ cup chicken stock

3 tablespoons fresh lemon juice

Salt

AVOCADO PUREE
½ cup fresh lime juice

1 cup crushed ice

2 serrano chiles

4 large avocados, peeled and seeded

1 bunch cilantro

2 tablespoons olive oil

Salt

To brine the yellowtail: In a blender, combine the salt, orange and lime zest, the bay leaves, and 4 cups of the water. Puree until the salt has dissolved. Transfer the brine to a container and add the remaining 6 cups water. Place the yellowtail in the brine and refrigerate for 30 minutes.

Meanwhile, make the salsa: In a large saucepan, heat enough canola oil to cover the bottom of the pan over medium heat. When hot, add the onions and cook, stirring, until they are browned and caramelized, 7 to 10 minutes. If they are not sizzling, increase the heat.

Char the habañero and halved peaches on a grill or over a gas burner until lightly blackened. If using stovetop burners, a long skewer will help here to turn the chiles without handling them. Do not touch your eyes.

When the onions are caramelized, add the chiles de árbol and ginger and cook over medium heat. Add the grilled habañero and peaches and stir to combine. Add the stock, bring to a simmer, and simmer for 2 minutes. Remove from the heat, add the lemon juice, and season with salt. Transfer the mixture to a blender. Carefully handling the hot mixture, puree until smooth, and transfer to a bowl to cool. Cover, and refrigerate to chill.

To make the avocado puree: Rinse out the blender. In the following order, add the lime juice, ice, serrano chiles, scooped flesh of the avocado, the cilantro, and olive oil, and puree until smooth. Season with salt.

Grill the fish: Oil the grill grates, then heat the grill to high (or heat a cast-iron pan over high heat). Remove the yellowtail from

CONTINUED

Baja Yellowtail Tostada with Peach-Habañero Salsa and Avocado Puree
CONTINUED

TO ASSEMBLE

2 handfuls of multicolor cherry tomatoes, halved

1 peach, pitted and cut into small dice

1 tablespoon olive oil

Juice of 1 lime

1 to 2 packages tostadas or tortillas

1 radish, shaved

Cilantro and cilantro blossoms, for garnish

Tiny mint leaves, for garnish

the brine and pat dry with a paper towel. Place the yellowtail on a plate and season well with salt and black pepper. Place the fish on the grill (or in the skillet) and sear for barely 2 minutes per side. You want the fish to be rare in the center but lightly charred. Transfer the yellowtail to a cutting surface and allow the fish to cool completely before cutting into sugar cube–size pieces.

To assemble: To really go for it, restaurant-style, load both the salsa and the puree into squirt bottles. In a large bowl, gently toss the diced fish with the cherry tomatoes, diced peach, olive oil, and lime juice until coated. Distribute the yellowtail mixture on top of each tostada and dollop artfully with the salsa and avocado. Garnish with radish medallions, cilantro, and mint. Serve immediately.

Angelini Osteria / Fig & Gorgonzola Gratin

Three ingredients. Ten minutes, start to finish. I wish I'd had this simple, decadent recipe then when the perfume of overripe figs used to announce the coming of autumn with every breeze through the Mission fig tree that lorded over the empty lot next to my old house in Venice. It's a classic cheese pairing turned to eleven. And it's straight from the culinary gospel of Gino Angelini. In the absence of saba, substitute your best balsamic vinegar.

SERVES 4 AS AN APPETIZER, 8 TO 10 AS HORS D'OEUVRES

12 fresh Black Mission figs

4 ounces Gorgonzola (blue) cheese

4 tablespoons saba (grape must reduction)

Preheat the broiler to 400°F.

Halve each fig lengthwise and place on a baking sheet, skin-side down. Crumble the Gorgonzola over each. Broil 3 to 5 minutes, until the cheese melts.

Divide figs among four plates. Drizzle each with 1 tablespoon of the saba and serve immediately.

Moon Juice / Cultured Nut Cheese

This Moon Juice staple by Amanda Chantal Bacon is a soft, lightly tangy spreading paste. Once it's fermented, you can portion it out and blend in saucy hints such as red chimichurri (page 59), or experiment with handfuls of herbes de Provence, shallots, and spring garlic; preserved lemon and Moroccan spices; even a fiery California sunset of lavender, chili oil, and honey. And, here, finally, here is where a deep pantry really shines—I have come to find adding flavors not wholly unlike choosing mix-ins for frozen yogurt.

MAKES 2 CUPS

1½ cups cashews
1 cup macadamia nuts
1 cup water
1 teaspoon probiotic powder

Put the cashews and macadamia nuts in separate bowls, add water to cover, and set aside to soak overnight. The next morning, drain and rinse.

Put the cashews, macadamias, and water in a blender and blend until smooth. Transfer the nut mixture to a glass container and add the probiotics; mix until thoroughly incorporated. Set the container in a dehydrator and hold at 90°F for 24 hours.

The following day, remove the nut cheese from the dehydrator and set aside to ferment, covered, at room temperature for another 48 hours. (You can use small molds, if you like.) Depending on how potent your probiotic is, and how warm your kitchen, the nut cheese will be of varying tanginess at the end of this period. Increasing its fermentation (air-curing) time will strengthen its flavor.

Refrigerate any leftover cheese; it will firm as it cures.

Café Gratitude / Garlic Tahini Sauce

Out of quieter beginnings up in San Francisco and its charmed entrance here in 2011, Café Gratitude has captured all the golden sunshine feelings that come with a (no-flesh but fleshed out) philosophy of plant-based wellness. The "I Am Whole, " its macrobiotic-inspired grain bowl that launched a thousand imitators, piles on that goodness. For many, the highlight of the dish is the accompanying ramekin of garlicky dressing, with its striking green color and whipped aioli-like consistency. Keep this satisfying sauce on hand for impromptu use as a dip, sandwich spread, or leftovers pick-me-up.

MAKES 2 CUPS

⅔ cup tahini
⅓ cup water
1 teaspoon salt
2 garlic cloves
⅓ cup fresh lemon juice
1 cup loosely packed fresh parsley leaves
⅔ cup olive oil

Puree the tahini, water, salt, and garlic in a blender. Scrape down the sides of the blender with a spatula and add the lemon juice and parsley. With the motor running, slowly drizzle in the olive oil. Don't overblend—make sure flecks of parsley are still visible in the dressing. Serve immediately, or refrigerate in an airtight container for up to 1 week.

Manhattan Beach Post / Red Chimichurri

Whether at his flagship restaurant M.B. Post or other neighborhood destinations like Fishing with Dynamite, chef/owner David LeFevre cares enough about condiments to offer not just homemade mustard but an entire flight of them. Thanks to a hit of brooding smoked paprika, he leaves the myth of bright-green chimichurri to greener pastures in favor of a rusty red. Chimichurri is supposed to be oily and a bit sour, and it may not win a beauty prize, but you can dip, drizzle, dunk, serve it alongside sausage or asado, or brush it across slabs of grilled rustic bread. Bonus: Chimichurri doesn't have to be fresh; actually, aged chimichurri is, well, a thing, and its vinegar content will stand up to plenty of fridge time.

MAKES ABOUT ¾ CUP

4 garlic cloves

¼ cup red wine vinegar

1 teaspoon smoked paprika

½ teaspoon red pepper flakes

½ teaspoon salt

½ cup olive oil

Leaves from ½ bunch parsley, chopped

Leaves from 3 oregano sprigs, chopped

Using a mortar and pestle, pound or process the garlic into a paste, then slowly add the vinegar. Once incorporated, add the paprika, red pepper flakes, and salt. (Or use a food processor, adding the ingredients all at once, then scrape down the sides.) With the machine running or while whisking, slowly drizzle in the olive oil to make a thick sauce. Transfer to a bowl and gently fold in the parsley and oregano.

HOMAGE TO THE AVOCADO TOAST

I have a good friend who spent two years off the grid in India. When he arrived home in late 2015, we gathered with friends, gorging ourselves on Korean bulgogi and bowls of glassy japchae.

We kept returning to that timeless question: whether the more things change in L.A., the more they stay the same.

> "For one, avocado toast is like, *a thing*," I said. "Restaurants are charging ten bucks for it."

He had missed the triumphant ascendancy of the humble avocado, on its toasted throne, into the kingdom of brunch.

> "How can it be a thing? You put avocado on toast. It's what you eat when there's nothing else to eat. Like PBJ."

This Santa Monica native had a point. Since our market falls on Wednesday, avocado on toast was previously relegated to lunch on Tuesday: leftover ripened avocado, lemon, red pepper flakes, olive oil on crisped heels of Bezian's sourdough, maybe topped with a fried egg.

His skepticism about a newfound ubiquity for delicious leftovers was understandable. A few weeks later, I received the text:

> "i see what u mean about the avo tst"

Re-claiming toasts and tartines for the home kitchen ought not be a difficult assimilation. After all, we've been eating avocado toast all along! We've only gotten a little fancier in formation. As a guide, we turn to artist Josef Albers. While he played with blocks of color in his Homage to the Square, here, the blocks are ingredients in *The L.A. Cookbook's* Homage to the Avocado Toast.

GO GET EM TIGER

Fried Egg

OSTRICH FARM

Crushed Red Chile
Meyer Lemon
Toasted Whole Wheat

BELLWETHER

Fried Egg
Aleppo Pepper

BLUE PLATE DINER

Fried Egg
Sun-Dried Tomato Relish

LODGE BREAD

Radish
Toasted Whole Wheat

SUPERBA FOOD + BREAD

Pickled Fresno Chile
Radish Sprouts
Cilantro

CECCONI'S

(Green) Eggs
Pesto
Toasted Multi-Grain

HART AND THE HUNTER

Pimiento
Hard-Boiled Egg
Smoked Trout

DINETTE

Crushed Red Chile
Meyer Lemon

VALERIE ECHO PARK

Pickled Asparagus
Fines Herbes
Lemon Confit

LITTLE PINE

Olive Oil
Meyer Lemon
Crushed Red Chile

GJELINA TAKEAWAY

Radish
Meyer Lemon
Sesame Seed

BAR MARMONT

Crab
Greens
(Smoked) Olive Oil

COMMISSARY AT THE LINE

Cured Salmon
Goat Cheese
Chilies

EVELEIGH

Cured Salmon
Chiles
Cilantro

GEORGIE

Poached Egg
Grilled Tomato
Pickled Onions

DESTROYER

Avocado Confit
Country Bread

PARAMOUNT COFFEE PROJECT

Cashew Butter
Fermented Salsa
Vegemite Sesame

TAR & ROSES

Pickled Onions
Sardine
Cilantro

JON & VINNY'S

Olive Oil
Meyer Lemon
Crushed Red Chile

AMARA KITCHEN

Salsa Verde
Pesto
Toasted Whole Wheat

ZINQUE

Tomato
Parmigiano Reggiano
Toasted Poilane

GRACIAS MADRE

Cashew Queso Blanco
Sprouts
Chiles

EVELEIGH

Espelette Pepper
Hard-Boiled Egg
Gribiche

LA CHAPTER AT ACE

Poached Egg
Aleppo Pepper
Toasted Seven-Grain

TERRINE

Tarragon
Salsa Verde
Radish

ROSE CAFE

Fried (Duck) Egg
Meyer Lemon
Pickled Fresno Pepper

SWINGERS

Olive Oil
Meyer Lemon
Crushed Red Chile

FREE RANGE

Over Easy Egg
Sriracha
Pickled Onions

LOVE & SALT

Tomato
Olive
Sherry Vinaigrette

enjoy life eat cake

MORNING BECOMES ECLECTIC

BREAKFAST AND BRUNCH

LocoL
Sweet & Creamy

Daughter's Granola
Candied Kumquat Almond Granola

Hatchet Hall
Fried Egg on Soft Polenta with Skillet Asparagus and Warm Virginia Ham Vinaigrette

Lucky Boy
Famous Breakfast Burrito

Porridge + Puffs
Rye & Teff Porridge with Cardamom-Caraway Caramel Apples,
Crispy Rosemary, Hazelnuts, and Cream

Maury's Bagels
Whitefish Salad

Wexler's Deli
Potato Latkes

Fountain Coffee Room
Silver Dollar Pancakes

Friends & Family
Cranberry Roly Poly

M Street Kitchen
Sourdough English Muffins

Cake Monkey Bakery
Gruyère-Thyme Monkey Breads

LocoL / Sweet & Creamy

The challenge at genre-bending concept LocoL is making foods and beverages irresistibly good, and inexpensive, without waste. First at Seattle's seminal Victrola, then at Intelligentsia in Silverlake, Tony "Tonx" Konecny's is now behind the dollar-a-cup coffee program at LocoL and house brand YES PLZ. He could not have teamed up with a better crew in Roy Choi, Daniel Patterson, and roastmaster Sumi Ali.

Traditional strong coffee brewed hot then served over ice preserves flavor but can run a bit bitter. For cold brew, coffee grounds steep in cold water over an extended period. The results offer sweetness and better mouthfeel, often at the expense of dimensionality—like cola gone flat. Playing around with ratios of the two, LocoL's mixture is ultimately tastier than each component on its own. The multi-step process is surprisingly easy.

MAKES 1 BATCH

3 parts brewed coffee, chilled
1 part cold brew concentrate
1 drop of vanilla extract (optional)

TO ASSEMBLE
2 parts half-and-half
1 part sweetened condensed milk
Ice

Brew the traditional coffee: For drip or pour-over coffee, use 8½ tablespoons (60 grams) of ground coffee per 4 cups (1 liter) filtered water. Brew according to your preferred method, then let cool. (In an airtight container, your coffee will keep in the fridge for a week.) To make the cold brew concentrate: Use a ratio of just over 1¼ cups (140 grams) of coarsely ground coffee per 4 cups (1 liter) of cold filtered water. That's about 5 tablespoons coffee per cup. Slowly pour the cold water into a French press or a carafe, pitcher, or mason jar, stirring as the coffee releases gas. Lightly cover with a kitchen towel and allow to steep for 12 to 14 hours on the counter.

Decant the concentrate into a clean container using a strainer, mesh colander, or careful pouring. To remove additional sediment, pour the concentrate through a paper filter. (The concentrate will keep in the refrigerator for 2 weeks.)

In a creamer or squeeze bottle, combine 2 parts half-and-half and 1 part sweetened condensed milk, plus the vanilla extract, if desired.

To make one Sweet & Creamy: Combine 3 parts chilled drip coffee with 1 part cold-brew concentrate over ice. Add the cream mixture to your desired coffee strength, and mix.

MASTERING COLD BREWING:

- Tonx recommends a burr grinder. Keep the cold-brew grind quite coarse. Pregrinding coffee in the store is heresy to most coffee nerds, but Tonx says it's less of a sin with cold coffee.

- To pour off the brew sans filter, a rice strainer, layered cheesecloth, or very clean cotton shirt are all worthy alternatives. You can create a cheesecloth "tea bag," too.

Daughter's Granola / Candied Kumquat Almond Granola

Emilie Coulson mixes her small-batch granola on Mondays, when husband Chef Carlos Delgado's celebrated Taco Maria restaurant in Costa Mesa is dark. On weekends, it's a star on the brunch menu, served with a yogurt mousse and decadent guava jam.

Once you nail down the ratios to this California staple, let your larder be your guide: Coarsely chop almonds one week; pistachios, the next. Add raisins, apricots, or dried persimmons. Swap the chia seed for basil seeds. If you like a clumpier granola, stir a whipped egg white into the mixture right before baking, then leave the cooked granola to cool overnight before breaking it up. For super-chewy and sweet, add 2 tablespoons light corn syrup and a bit of nut butter. Bonus: Save leftover kumquat simple syrup for fresh sodas and cocktail mixers.

MAKES 1 POUND

CANDIED KUMQUATS
½ pint (6 ounces) fresh kumquats or tangerines
½ cup sugar
1 cup water

GRANOLA
¾ cup raw almonds
2 cups rolled oats
⅓ cup chia seeds
¾ cup large coconut flakes
5 tablespoons maple syrup
2 tablespoons canola oil
Salt

To make the candied kumquats: Slice the fruit crosswise into slices the thickness of a quarter (about ¹⁄₁₆ inch). Carefully remove any seeds, keeping the rounds intact.

In a small saucepan, heat the sugar and water, stirring occasionally, until the sugar has dissolved. Remove from the heat, add the kumquat slices, and let steep for 1 hour.

Preheat the oven to 175°F (alternately, use a food dehydrator set to 135°F). Line a baking sheet with parchment paper. Using a slotted spoon, remove the kumquats from the simple syrup and spread them over the sheet. Bake for 75 minutes, then flip each slice and bake for 10 minutes more. You want them dehydrated, but their consistency can be anywhere between pliable and crisp, depending on your taste. Remove from the oven and set aside. Increase the oven temperature to 300°F.

To make the granola: Coarsely chop the almonds, and then mix with the oats, chia seeds, and coconut flakes in a large bowl. Add the maple syrup and canola oil and combine thoroughly. Season with salt.

Line a baking sheet with parchment paper. Spread the granola mixture evenly over the baking sheet, patting down with a spatula to keep it firm. Toast in the oven until the granola reaches a deep golden brown color. After 30 minutes, check every 5 to 10 minutes so the coconut doesn't burn—you want to still see some white on the flakes.

Remove the toasted granola from the oven and without handling it, let the pieces continue to firm. Once cooled, mix the kumquats into the granola.

Store in a sealed container at room temperature for up to 6 weeks, or freeze it, if you'd like.

Hatchet Hall / Fried Egg on Soft Polenta with Skillet Asparagus and Warm Virginia Ham Vinaigrette

Axe, Wolf in Sheep's Clothing, Hart & The Hunter, and now with Hatchet Hall in Culver City—Georgia native Brian Dunsmoor's Southern-inflected cooking has been an L.A. staple for years. When planning a brunch for hearty eaters, consider this serious egg skillet as Lowcountry cooking by way of California.

Polenta leftovers are like magic clay. Cool the finished polenta on a baking sheet, then slice and toast polenta fries to go with Ammo ketchup (page 167), smear broiled squares with Garlic Tahini Sauce (page 56) and feta, or add a little water to reheat and serve with a rustic ragù (page 116).

SERVES 6

VIRGINIA HAM VINAIGRETTE
1 cup diced country ham
3 tablespoons minced shallot
¼ cup bacon fat (not lard)
2 cups ham hock stock or chicken stock
½ cup apple cider vinegar
1 tablespoon whole-grain mustard
¼ cup olive oil
Salt

POLENTA
3 cups water
1 cup heavy cream
Dash of salt
1 cup fresh polenta, stone-ground cornmeal, or antebellum grits
2 tablespoons butter, in two pieces
Freshly ground black pepper

TO ASSEMBLE
2 tablespoons rendered country-ham fat, bacon fat, or olive oil
1 or 2 bunches pencil asparagus (about 36 spears) or 24 jumbo asparagus spears
6 large eggs
Salt and freshly ground black pepper
Shaved Parmesan, for garnish
Chopped fresh herbs (parsley, chervil, dill, green onion, tarragon, chive batons), for garnish

To make the vinaigrette: In a saucepan, render the ham with the shallots in the bacon fat over medium-high heat for about 5 minutes. Add the stock, lower the heat slightly, and bring to a simmer. Once the liquid has reduced by half, add the vinegar and mustard and whisk in the olive oil very slowly. Season with salt. Keep warm over low heat.

To make the polenta: In a stockpot, bring the water and cream to a boil over medium heat. Add the salt. While whisking, slowly add the polenta. Return to a boil, then lower the heat and simmer for 45 minutes for very soft polenta or up to 1 hour for a firmer consistency. The key is to stir diligently and thoroughly with a wooden spoon. Don't be fooled if the polenta seems done after only a few minutes—stopping now will result in gritty, underdone polenta. Keep stirring, and as it cooks, watch the sides to make sure they don't dry out (stir in a little more liquid if they do). Finish by whisking in the butter until smooth. Season with salt and pepper, and set aside. Cover to keep warm.

To assemble: Set out 6 plates and spoon ½ cup hot polenta onto each. In a cast-iron skillet, heat the ham fat until almost smoking. Add the asparagus and sear on all sides until just charred in spots but still bright green and crunchy, and divide among the plates, on top of the polenta.

Working quickly, wipe out the skillet and add another splash of oil. Over medium-high heat, gently crack in the eggs, one at a time (you can do these in two batches, if easier). Adjust the heat so the eggs sizzle but the fat doesn't splatter, and cook just till the whites are set but the yolks remain runny. Season with salt and pepper. Using a spatula, remove each finished egg to one of the waiting plates.

Drizzle 2 tablespoons of the ham vinaigrette over each plate and garnish each with a shave of Parmesan and a handful of herbs. Serve immediately.

Lucky Boy / Famous Breakfast Burrito

Born out of a worker's need to bring something easy and nourishing to take along to farms and factories, the chief intent for the burrito has always been hearty portable sustenance. Case in point: Lucky Boy's bestseller. It technically serves one, but that doesn't specify for how many days! This behemoth of egg, seasoned hash browns, cheese, bacon, and a plethora of add-ins (I go for chorizo and avocado) remains the centerpiece of this decades-old Pasadena greasy spoon directly across from the original Trader Joe's. Feel free to use ready-made hash browns or a shredded take on Wexler's latke recipe (page 75).

MAKES 1

5 slices bacon
1 extra-large flour tortilla
2 tablespoons butter
1½ cups hash browns
½ teaspoon paprika
¼ teaspoon chopped garlic
¼ teaspoon salt, plus more for the eggs
¼ teaspoon freshly ground black pepper, plus more for the eggs
3 extra-large eggs
½ cup grated cheddar or Monterey Jack cheese
Salsa (see page 38), for dipping

In a cast-iron skillet over medium heat, fry the bacon just till crisp, or bake in a 350°F oven for 12 to 18 minutes. Set aside on a rack or paper towel–lined plate. Heat a griddle or wipe out the skillet and put back over medium-low heat. Warm the tortilla on the griddle or cast-iron skillet, about 30 seconds on each side. Set aside.

In a second skillet, melt 1 tablespoon butter over medium heat. Add the hash browns, paprika, chopped garlic, salt, and pepper and cook until the hash browns are golden, about 5 minutes. Set aside.

Wipe out the skillet and heat the remaining 1 tablespoon butter over medium-low. Crack the eggs into a bowl and beat with salt and pepper to taste (add a splash of milk if you like fluffier eggs). Pour the beaten eggs into the skillet, shaking the pan and using a rubber spatula or wooden spoon to continually jostle the eggs, forming soft, creamy curds. Quickly remove from the heat.

To assemble: Mound the hash browns across the center of the griddled tortilla in a thick line, leaving space at either end. Top with the scrambled eggs and sprinkle with cheese. Lay the bacon on top of the eggs. Fold both sides of the tortilla inward toward the center, as if wrapping a present. Holding these down, bring the bottom edge up and over the filling. Tuck this edge and, holding the sides steady, roll the burrito away from you.

Place the rolled burrito in the center of two overlapping sheets of parchment paper and repeat the process, folding in the sides of the parchment, tucking the bottom edge over the burrito, and rolling securely. Slice the wrapped burrito in half and serve with salsa.

Porridge + Puffs / Rye & Teff Porridge with Cardamom-Caraway Caramel Apples, Crispy Rosemary, Hazelnuts, and Cream

This rich autumn porridge is cooked into dry, crispy clumps, then bathed in a generous splash of cream, seasonal compote, and nuts—and it even packs in the caffeine. Roving porridge maven Minh Phan, a resident veteran of the pop-up, serves this decadent bowl with roasted halved hazelnuts and aromatic sprigs of fried rosemary. Whole-grain teff and rye beer add a malty, bubbly feel with earthy ground notes. Think of this recipe as a flexible, interchangeable base for layering flavors and textures by varying the grains (4 cups), liquid (8 to 10 cups), and toppings. It's also handy to freeze chunks of porridge for hearty breakfasts on the fly.

SERVES 4 TO 6

PORRIDGE

1 cup dry red currants

2 cups rye stout or other stout/ porter, milk, or water

2 cups teff or other small grain, such as amaranth

1½ cups steel-cut oats (not quick-cooking)

1 cup medium-grain brown rice (such as Koda Farm's Kokuho Rose)

¼ cup whole-grain rye

¼ cup black sweet rice or forbidden rice

¼ cup millet

2 cups strong black coffee, milk, or water

5 cups whole milk or nondairy milk (such as almond or rice milk), plus more as needed

¾ cup packed brown sugar

2 teaspoons salt

CARDAMOM-CARAWAY CARAMELIZED APPLE COMPOTE

1 lemon

4 to 6 tart and sweet apples, such as Pink Lady or Braeburn

1 cup (2 sticks) butter, cubed

½ cup packed brown sugar

½ cup granulated sugar

2 teaspoons ground cardamom

2 teaspoons caraway seeds

½ teaspoon grated nutmeg

½ teaspoon salt

To make the porridge: In a small bowl, rehydrate the currants in the rye stout for at least 20 minutes.

Put the teff, oats, brown rice, rye, sweet rice, and millet in a large, shallow saucepan. Shake and stir the pan over medium heat for 2 to 3 minutes, until toasty and aromatic. Stir in the currants with their soaking liquid. Simmer until the liquid has evaporated, another 2 minutes or so. Pour in the coffee and keep the mixture at a simmer. When most of the coffee has been absorbed and the grains begin to plump, after about 4 minutes, add the milk, brown sugar, and salt and stir well. Reduce the heat to low, cover, and cook for 10 to 30 minutes more (depending on the grains you use), until the liquid has been completely absorbed and the grains are al dente. If they're not, simply add more milk.

Remove from the heat and let cool, uncovered, so the porridge dries out. You can also spread it out in a baking pan. (The time-crunched or impatient can eat this right away with a splash of cream on top.)

To make the compote: Fill a large bowl with water and juice the lemon into the bowl. Peel the apples and cut them into thin wedges, placing them in the water as you go.

In a large saucepan, melt ½ cup (1 stick) of the butter over medium heat. Drain and pat dry the apples and add them to the pan. Cook, stirring well, for 2 to 3 minutes. Stir in both sugars until thoroughly incorporated. Add the remaining ½ cup (1 stick) butter, the cardamom, caraway, nutmeg, and salt and cook until the mixture is a caramel color and has a syrupy, loose consistency, about 5 minutes. (The compote can be prepared ahead, chilled, and reheated. Add a pat or two of butter when warming to loosen it.)

To assemble: Preheat the broiler. Line a wire rack with paper towels. In a small saucepan, heat just enough vegetable oil to cover the rosemary to 350°F. Break the rosemary into short lengths and

CONTINUED

Rye & Teff Porridge with Cardamom-Caraway Caramel Apples, Crispy Rosemary, Hazelnuts, and Cream

CONTINUED

TO ASSEMBLE
Vegetable oil, for frying
4 to 6 rosemary sprigs
Heavy cream, for serving
½ cup roasted or toasted hazelnuts, halved or chopped

carefully add them to the oil. Fry just till crisp, about 30 seconds, in batches if need be. Using a slotted spoon, quickly transfer them to the rack.

Break up or score the porridge into chunks and place on a rimmed baking sheet. Broil for a few minutes, just till the edges crisp.

Divide the porridge chunks among bowls. Add a generous splash of cream, a spoonful of compote, a sprinkle of nuts, and finish with the fried rosemary.

Maury's Bagels / Whitefish Salad

Jason Kaplan has filtered East Coast nostalgia through a California food lens—one sharpened during his years at both Gjelina Take Away and Gjusta in Venice. The result is a lovingly hand-rolled bagel, baked in micro batches. After slathering on the cream cheese, a whitefish bagel isn't without shaved red onion and a layer of Jason's quick pickles. He slices Persian cucumbers thinly on a mandoline, sprinkles them with a small amount of sugar, then splashes on the vinegar and tosses. There you have it: instant seasoned cukes that will hold for a few days in an airtight container.

SERVES 4 TO 6

1 pound high-quality smoked whitefish

½ cup labneh (or yogurt, sour cream, dairy-free Kite Hill cheese)

1 tablespoon cream cheese (or dairy-free Kite Hill cream cheese)

1 tablespoon minced green onion

1½ teaspoons finely chopped dill

Zest of ½ lemon

1½ teaspoons fresh lemon juice

¼ to ½ teaspoon finely grated horseradish (fresh or jarred)

Freshly ground black pepper

Put all the ingredients in a bowl and combine with a fork, but not to a total mush. Keep an eye out for, and remove, any bones. Keep refrigerated in an airtight container for up to two to three days.

TO
SANTA MONICA
HOT!
OG!
BIG POPPA!
LA
RAMS
LOX.
ROOT BEER
THE UNCLE LEO!
Wexler's
M.
"HEY! HEY! SMOKE FISH EVERY DAY!"
SCHMEAR!
FRESH!
M.
CREAM SODA
DELI
M
CORNED BEEF.

Wexler's Deli / Potato Latkes

L.A.'s deli renaissance is a revival of traditions and artisanal methods that, along with Yiddish and kreplach, might not survive otherwise. Micah Wexler's credo of smoking fish every day encapsulates the modern movement: fresher, newer, more immediate. Come holiday, potato pancakes get the farmers' market treatment, too.

At least one of Hanukkah's eight nights is spent arguing with family about applesauce versus sour cream/crème fraîche as a dipping side for latkes. (There's inevitably a ketchup heathen in the bunch.) No matter what tribe you fall in, feel free to load it on.

MAKES ABOUT 24 LATKES

1¼ pounds Yukon Gold potatoes (about 4)
1 white onion, quartered
Table salt
2 eggs
1 cup all-purpose flour
Freshly ground black pepper
Vegetable oil, for frying

In a food processor, shred the potatoes and then the onion. After a first shredding, run the mixture through the processor a second time.

Place a large stockpot of salted water to boil. Fill a large bowl with ice and water. Once boiling, add the potato-onion mixture and blanch for 45 seconds. Immediately drain and plunge into the ice bath. Using a kitchen towel, squeeze the daylights out of the mixture and lay it out on a baking sheet. (This part will be messy; best to do it over a large bowl or near the sink.) Place the baking sheet in the refrigerator to cool.

Beat the eggs in a large bowl. Add the cooled potato-onion mixture and stir to combine. Mix in the flour. Season with salt and pepper.

In a large cast-iron skillet, heat a ¼-inch layer of vegetable oil over medium heat. Form the latkes by hand, about the size of your palm and not too thick (or they won't cook through). Carefully drop the latkes into the hot oil. Don't crowd them, or the temperature of the oil will drop and the latkes won't brown as well. Cook on each side for 3 minutes, or until strongly golden and crispy. Remove and drain on a wire rack set over paper towels. Serve immediately.

Fountain Coffee Room / Silver Dollar Pancakes

Steeped in endless bungalow lore, Sunset Boulevard's landmark Beverly Hills Hotel remains every bit the ingénue's daydream of bright red lips and black-and-white pictures, impossibly turquoise pools and salads and palm frond wallpaper framing the Fountain Coffee Room's curvaceous counter. We can't predict the future, so it's nice to know some things, like the silver-dollar pancakes and that pink-and-green Martinique wallpaper, feel timeless. Griddled to a buttery crisp, the pancakes remain exceptionally fluffy thanks to the loving step of beating the egg whites to a meringue-like consistency—almost like a whipped beauty cream for a screen siren. Give it a try. Or have the cabana boy do it.

SERVES 4

1 ¾ cups all-purpose flour
2 teaspoons baking soda
1 tablespoon sugar
1 teaspoon salt
2 cups buttermilk
½ cup (1 stick) butter, melted
2 eggs, separated
Butter, for serving
Maple syrup, for serving
Powdered sugar, for serving

Set out three bowls. In the first, mix the flour, baking soda, sugar, and salt together. In the second, mix the buttermilk, melted butter, and egg yolks. In the third bowl, using a whisk (or in a stand mixer fitted with the whisk attachment), whip the egg whites until they hold stiff peaks.

Add the buttermilk mixture to the flour mixture and mix just until incorporated.

Using a spatula, gently fold in the egg whites. Refrigerate the batter for at least 10 minutes.

Melt a dab of butter over medium heat in a griddle or cast-iron pan and swirl it around. Spoon the batter out using a 2-ounce ladle, being careful not to overcrowd the pan (the batter will spread). Cook for about 2 minutes; when you see bubbles forming through the center, flip. The color should be deep golden brown. One minute later, remove the pancake to your stack. Keep stacks warm in the oven, or at the table under foil.

Coat with butter, maple syrup, and a sprinkle of powdered sugar.

Friends & Family / Cranberry Roly Poly

If you love breakfast pastries like *rugelach* and scones, you'll dig this. Friends & Family baker Roxana Jullapat began with the *Fanny Farmer Cookbook* for this time-honored pastry filled with jam and rolled into a pinwheel shape. Instead of traditional pie dough as the vehicle for the vanilla-scented cranberry jam, the pastry chef has chosen a barely sweetened scone-ish dough. The pinwheel caps a holiday dinner with a scoop of vanilla as easily as it satisfies breakfast pastry fans, especially when paired with a Sweet & Creamy (page 65).

MAKES 8

CRANBERRY JAM
1 cup sugar
½ cup water
1 vanilla bean
1 pound fresh or frozen cranberries (about 3 cups)

DOUGH
2¼ cups (313 grams) all-purpose flour, sifted
⅓ cup (67 grams) granulated sugar
1 tablespoon baking powder
¾ cup (170 grams) cold butter, cubed
½ cup (50 grams) candied ginger, cut into small dice
¼ cup (30 grams) dried cranberries
¾ cup (175 grams) heavy cream, plus 2 tablespoons for brushing
Decorating crystal sugar, for sprinkling

To make the cranberry jam: In a heavy-bottomed pot, combine the sugar and water, but do not stir. Using a paring knife, split the vanilla bean lengthwise, scrape out the seeds and pulp, and stir both the seeds and scraped bean into the pot. Bring to a boil over high heat and cook till the mixture turns translucent—this won't take more than a few minutes—then lower the heat to medium-low. The syrup will reduce, taking on a golden color as it thickens.

Carefully stir the cranberries into the hot syrup, and cook till it reaches a jammy consistency, stirring continuously with a wooden spoon. You'll hear the cranberries pop, so don't put your face near the pot. After about 2 minutes, the jam will foam up and take on the fruit's color. Keep stirring for 5 to 7 minutes more as it thickens.

To test the jam: Spoon a bit of jam onto a cold plate or glass dish, and brush it with your finger. If your finger leaves a trace, the jam is ready. If not, cook for a bit longer and test again.

Remove and discard the vanilla bean. Transfer the jam to a bowl to cool. (The jam will keep in the refrigerator for up to a month; if you're a savvy preserver, you may jar it now to extend its shelf life.)

To make the dough: In a bowl, combine the flour, sugar, and baking powder. Toss in the butter. Using a pastry cutter or your fingertips, and working quickly, break up the butter into dime-size pieces. Add the candied ginger and dried cranberries. Using your hands, mix gently until just combined. Make a well in the center. Pour in the cream. Gently knead until the dough comes together.

Line a clean work surface with a rectangle of plastic wrap, about 12 inches long by 14 inches wide. Transfer the dough to the plastic wrap. Using a rolling pin, flatten the dough into a rectangle about 8½ inches long by 12 inches wide. If the dough is sticky, dust the rolling pin lightly with flour. Using a spatula, spread 1 cup of the cranberry jam on top of the dough, leaving a ½-inch border around the edges.

To roll, lift the bottom end of the plastic wrap and lightly roll the jam-covered dough into a log away from you, like a jelly roll. Wrap

CONTINUED

Cranberry Roly Poly

the rolled log tightly in plastic. Chill in the freezer for 1 to 2 hours, until firm but not completely frozen (this will help with slicing).

To bake the roll: Preheat the oven to 350°F. Line two baking sheets with parchment paper. Lightly coat the parchment paper with nonstick spray.

Unwrap the log. Using a sharp chef's knife, slice it crosswise into 8 pinwheels, about 1½ inches thick. Thicker slices, once baked, will more resemble a scone; thinner, a cookie. Place four pinwheels on each prepared baking sheet, at least 2 inches apart. Using a pastry brush, paint each pinwheel with the remaining cream, and sprinkle with the crystal sugar.

Bake for 20 to 28 minutes, until golden brown. For the first 10 minutes, the dough will stay mostly flat, as if baking a sugar cookie, before puffing up. By 15 minutes, light cracks and the very beginnings of color should start to show. Let cool completely on the baking sheets before serving.

M Street Kitchen / Sourdough English Muffins

Says Chef Jeff Mahin, "A sourdough starter is like a houseplant. If you forget to feed it, it will die." Indeed, naturally leavened English muffins begin with welcoming the daily rhythms of sourdough starter into your life. Once that's under control, the rest is process: Pre-chill the bowl, mix the dough the night before, get a full night's sleep, proof, and finish in time for brunch. Chef Mahin says the two keys to success are keeping the bowl cold, and checking that anytime the dough's temperature rises above about 75°F, to chill it for five minutes and then proceed as directed. M Street Kitchen in Santa Monica serves these oversize griddled joys as part of a "commuter" egg sandwich, and they're excellent on their own with fresh preserves.

When griddling the muffins, clarified butter (ghee is a version) has the high smoke point that gives it endurance in heat applications. The muffins sit on the hot cast-iron for some time, and most oils and fats, including regular butter, can't stand up to this. Clarifying the butter– removing the milk proteins and water–ensures you won't ruin all your work on the final step.

MAKES 12

SOURDOUGH STARTER

1 bunch unwashed organic grapes (preferably from a local farmers' market)

100 grams filtered water, plus more for feeding the starter

100 grams (¾ cup plus 2½ teaspoons) unbleached all-purpose flour, plus more for feeding the starter

ENGLISH MUFFINS

480 grams (2 cups) sourdough starter (see above)

335 grams (1⅖ cups) filtered water, chilled to 58°F

395 grams (3⅓ cups) bread flour (14% protein)

167 grams (1⅖ cups) all-purpose flour

14 grams (2½ teaspoons) sea salt

Cornmeal or rice flour, for dusting

Butter (or ghee) for clarifying

To begin the sourdough starter: Wrap the grapes in cheesecloth or a nut-milk bag. Place the grapes in a bowl and add the water. Using your hands, lightly crush the grapes in the cloth, then slosh with the water for 3 minutes. Set aside on a plate. Add the flour to the bowl and mix until well combined. Return the grapes and cover the bowl with additional cheesecloth, securing it with rubber bands or string until taut.

Allow the starter to sit out at room temperature (at least 72°F) for 2 to 3 days. You'll be looking for bubbles–a sign of fermentation–and a sweet, grapey smell that will replace the more neutral scent of flour. Remove and discard both the grapes and any water that has collected on top of the starter.

To feed the starter daily: You'll use equal parts starter, water, and flour. Measure out 100 grams of the starter and mix with 100 grams filtered water and 100 grams unbleached all-purpose flour. Mix by hand until a clumpy dough begins to form. Place this back into a large bowl, cover with cheesecloth, and allow to sit at room temperature for another 24 hours, near an open window to maximize the natural yeasts. Continue this process daily for the next 4 days. Each day, you'll measure out 100 grams of the starter, discarding the rest, feed the starter with 100 grams water and 100 grams flour, mix well with your hands, replace the cover, and return it to its place. The idea is to get a sweet, fermented smell that's not too vinegary. This is your active starter.

When the starter has an active rhythm going and smells sweet, you can build up the 480 grams you need for the muffins.

CONTINUED

Sourdough English Muffins

Continue to pour out the 200 grams, and add a 1:1 ratio of flour and water in increasing amounts. Each day you must feed the starter. Once it is active, you only need to leave it out for 1 to 2 hours, then it can live in the refrigerator.

The day before you plan to mix your dough: Chill the bowl of a stand mixer.

The next day, in the chilled mixer bowl, combine the 480 grams of the starter, water, the bread flour, all-purpose flour, and salt. Set a timer and mix for 5 minutes on low speed until the dough is pale and smooth. Place a damp dishcloth or plastic wrap over the bowl and let rest for 20 minutes.

Mix for 1 to 2 minutes on medium speed. The dough should begin to make slapping sounds. As the gluten becomes more developed, the slapping sounds should increase in frequency. It should begin to appear smooth with a slight sheen to it, and the dough should begin to pull away from the sides and bottom of the bowl.

Test for gluten development with a windowpane check: Using wet hands, hold up and spread out a small piece of dough between fingers to see if it will stretch without breaking. It should stretch well and be translucent. If it breaks, the gluten hasn't developed sufficiently yet.

Lightly grease a large glass bowl with nonstick spray or oil. Place the dough in the bowl, cover with plastic wrap, and set on the counter at room temperature. Set a timer for 45 minutes.

To shape the muffins: After 45 minutes, turn out the dough onto a lightly floured work surface. Sprinkle a baking sheet generously with cornmeal. Using a digital scale and bench knife, portion 115 grams of dough for each muffin. Without overworking, lightly fold each portion into a ball. Place each shaped ball on the baking sheet. Cover the completed dozen with plastic wrap. Refrigerate for at least 8 hours, or overnight.

To proof the muffins: The next morning, pull out the baking sheet. Set aside in a warm spot to proof for 1 to 1½ hours, until each muffin is about 3½ inches in diameter.

You can use ready-made ghee or, while you're proofing, clarify butter to keep the dough from scorching when in the griddle: In a small saucepan, gently melt the butter over the lowest heat and watch until it stops bubbling. You'll see white appear, get frothy, separate, and ultimately dissolve. Once the bubbling stops, remove any skin that has formed on the surface and pour the yellow fat through a strainer—this is the clarified butter.

To griddle the muffins: Heat a cast-iron skillet or griddle over medium heat for 3 minutes. Add just enough ghee or clarified butter to coat the griddle—you want to griddle the muffins, not fry them. Working with 2 at a time, cook the muffins on the griddle until the surface on each side is golden brown, at least 4 minutes per side to fully cook through. The muffins will puff a bit when they hit the heat. Using a spatula, press down gently to slightly flatten the muffins and flip. The muffins are done when crisp and no longer gummy around the sides. Remove with a spatula and cool fully on a rack. Dust finished muffins with cornmeal.

To serve: Fork-split the sides and pull apart. The muffins are best when toasted. (Baked muffins will keep for up to 3 days in a plastic bag, or frozen for longer.)

Cake Monkey Bakery / Gruyère-Thyme Monkey Breads

Whereas pull-apart monkey breads often skew cinnamon-roll sweet, Elizabeth Belkind has rethought the croissant-dough pastry with savory sophistication. Don't let the *length* of this recipe deter you; Cake Monkey's luncheon-ready treats just take a few extra words to describe. The active time and technique isn't excruciating, but the timeline is formidable: a first night to mix the poolish; a short period the next day to mix the dough and roll out the butter; intervals the next day to laminate and rest the dough; and a final rise before baking.

The recipe calls for bread flour, which has higher protein content than all-purpose flour and develops gluten faster to give the pastry a lighter, springier texture. You'll also need round 3½-inch-diameter x 1½-inch-tall waxed paper molds found online or at baking-supply stores. As this recipe yields 20, Belkind suggests freezing half the dough for shaping into croissants or *pains au chocolat*.

MAKES 20

POOLISH STARTER

3 cups plus 1¾ tablespoons (395 grams) bread flour

1⅔ cups (395 grams) water, at room temperature

½ teaspoon (1 gram) instant yeast (not active dry)

DOUGH

1⅓ cups (308 grams) milk, at room temperature

¾ cup (168 grams) plus 1 tablespoon sugar

1 tablespoon plus 1 teaspoon (13 grams) instant yeast (not active dry)

¼ cup (52 grams) butter, melted and cooled

7 cups plus 2 tablespoons (905 grams) bread flour, plus more for dusting

1 tablespoon plus 2 teaspoons (26 grams) and a pinch of Morton kosher salt

2¼ cups (4½ sticks or 18 ounces) European-style butter (minimum of 83% butterfat content), cold but soft

2¼ pounds Gruyère cheese, grated, plus additional for garnish

1¼ cups thyme leaves

4 eggs

2 egg yolks

Prepare the poolish the night before you'd like to make your dough: In a small bowl, mix the bread flour, water, and instant yeast, breaking up any clumps. Set aside for at least 8 hours.

To make the dough: The next day, combine the poolish, milk, ¾ cup of the sugar, and the yeast in the bowl of a stand mixer fitted with the dough hook. Stir for 30 seconds. With the machine running, add the melted butter, then the flour and salt. Mix on low speed for 4 to 5 minutes.

To test if your dough is ready, pull a small handful and stretch it between your hands. It should be soft and pliable, and stretch without tearing, like a balloon. If the dough doesn't stretch, or if it tears when you pull it apart, mix it for 1 to 2 minutes more and test again.

Line a baking sheet with parchment paper and coat the paper with nonstick spray. Turn the dough out onto the baking sheet. Cover the dough with plastic wrap or a slightly dampened cloth, and refrigerate overnight, making sure no part of the surface of the dough is exposed to air.

Meanwhile, place a piece of parchment paper on a clean work surface and draw a 12 by 6-inch rectangle on the parchment. Flip the parchment over.

Fit the stand mixer with the paddle attachment and beat the European-style butter on low speed for about 5 minutes, until soft and lighter in color. Turn the butter out onto the parchment. Using a spatula, shape the butter so it fills the drawn rectangle. Fold the sides of the parchment up to enclose the butter. Use a rolling pin to flatten the butter, making sure there are no pockets of air left (this will ensure even lamination in your dough). Cover with parchment paper or plastic wrap, then refrigerate until solid.

CONTINUED

Gruyère-Thyme Monkey Breads

After the dough has rested overnight, about 1 hour before you are ready to turn the dough, remove the rolled butter from the refrigerator. Before you begin, make sure both the dough and the butter block are the same firmness and temperature. (Return either to the freezer briefly to firm up or knead lightly with the rolling pin to soften.) Dust the dough with flour and set it on a floured work surface. Roll out into a rectangle about 19 by 7 inches. Place the butter directly on top, leaving a ½-inch border of dough on the three sides nearest to you, and a 6½ by 7-inch rectangle of exposed dough on the side farthest from you.

Starting away from you, fold the exposed edge of dough in over the butter, covering half. Then fold the side nearest you up over the folded dough in the opposite direction, to create an even packet with five layers: dough-butter-dough-butter-dough.

Press the edges together to encase the butter, and, using the rolling pin, roll the folded dough back out into a rectangle about 19 by 7 inches. Return the dough to the baking sheet, cover again, and refrigerate for 30 more minutes.

Perform the first turn: Place the rectangle of dough on the work surface so the seam is closest to your right hand. Press lightly with a large rolling pin at all edges to flatten. Roll the dough gently about ½ inch thick into a rectangle about 20 by 12 inches wide. Fold into thirds like a letter. Place on the baking sheet, cover completely, and refrigerate for 1½ to 2 hours, until chilled but pliable again.

Perform the second and third turns: Repeat these steps two more times, refrigerating the dough for 1½ to 2 hours between each turn. After the third turn, roll the dough out to about ¼-inch thickness. The dough is now complete. Cover and refrigerate it for at least 8 hours before assembling and baking.

To assemble the monkey breads: Let the dough sit at room temperature for a few minutes. Roll the dough out into a 20 by 12-inch rectangle about ¼ inch thick. Divide the dough into two portions, one weighing 4¼ pounds and the other weighing 2½ pounds (chill any remaining dough for another use). Cover and refrigerate the 2½-pound portion.

Using a pizza cutter, cut the larger portion of dough into ½-inch cubes. In a bowl, toss the cubes with 1¼ pounds of the grated cheese and about three quarters of the thyme leaves. Arrange the waxed paper molds onto baking sheets. Place about 3½ ounces of the cheesy dough mixture into each mold. Set aside in a warm area.

Remove the smaller piece of dough from the refrigerator and, using a pizza cutter, cut into ¼-inch-thick strips about 12 inches long. Sprinkle these with the remaining cheese and thyme. Working from the farthest edge, roll each strip toward you into a tight spiral, leaving a ½-inch tab at the end. Fold this tab over the spiral to secure the shape. Top each paper mold with one spiral.

Allow the breads to rise in a warm spot, uncovered, until they roughly double in size. This time will vary from kitchen to kitchen. (It shouldn't be so warm that the butter begins to melt and seep out of the dough.) Preheat the oven to 350°F.

In a small bowl, whisk the eggs, egg yolks, a pinch of salt, and the remaining 1 tablespoon sugar. Use a pastry brush to paint the top of each monkey bread with the egg wash.

Divide the breads between two baking sheets. Bake one sheet for about 13 minutes, then rotate and bake for 10 to 13 minutes more, until the tops are a beautiful dark burnished brown. Repeat with the second baking sheet. Allow the monkey breads to cool briefly before serving.

HOLLYWOOD BOWL

SOUPS, STEWS, AND BOWLS

Belcampo Meat Co.
Bone Broth

Greenspan's Grilled Cheese
Tomato-Basil Soup

Heirloom L.A.
Grilled Pear Gazpacho with Parmesan Cheese Crisps and Red Endive–Walnut Salad

Croft Alley
Pho Ga (Chicken Pho)

Orsa & Winston
Red Kuri Squash Soup with Yuzu Koshō Crème Fraîche

Winsome
Charred Escarole Chicken Stew

Ricebar
Bisteg Tagalog (Rice Bowl with Soy and Calamansi–Marinated Beef)

Lincoln
Farro Bowl with Baby Kale, Smoky Chickpeas, Charred Lemon, and Romesco

Patina
Artichoke Velouté

MANUFACTURED
by
BELCAMPO® FARMS
4720 SCARFACE RD GAZELLE CA 96034

Try some...

Bone Broth

28 oz net wt.
794 GRAMS, PERISHABLE
KEEP REFRIGERATED

...ARMS
...LE CA 96034

Broth

MANUFACTURED
by
BELCAMPO® FARMS
4720 SCARFACE RD GAZELLE CA 96034

Try some...

Bone Broth

28 oz net wt.
794 GRAMS, PERISHABLE
KEEP REFRIGERATED

...ED
...FARMS
...LE CA 96034

Broth

Belcampo Meat Co. / Bone Broth

It stands to reason that arguably the best, and most gorgeous butchery in the country would make a mean bone broth. Belcampo keeps their stock going 24/7, available piping hot in takeaway cups at their Santa Monica location. The nourishing elixir is also available in cute pint or quart containers from the freezer, which at first glance could be mistaken for ice cream. Prank potential aside, Eastern medicine has a long tradition of rejuvenating bone broths for everything from fortifying postnatal moms to warding off depression. Delicious to sip and a spectacular base for many dishes, Anya Fernald's simple recipe will ensure you have a steady supply on hand.

MAKES ABOUT 1 QUART

4 pounds assorted bones (beef, pork, lamb)
4 quarts filtered water

FOR EACH PORTION
½ teaspoon fresh lime juice
½ teaspoon chile-garlic sauce
¼ teaspoon salt
or
½ teaspoon ginger juice
½ teaspoon turmeric juice

Preheat the oven to 450°F.

Place the bones on a baking sheet and roast until they are a rich dark golden brown, about 30 minutes, depending on the size of the bones. Remove the bones and transfer to an extra-large stockpot. Submerge them in the filtered water. Simmer over low heat for up to 48 hours. (The broth will be more concentrated the longer it simmers.)

Remove from the heat and allow to cool in the stockpot. Give a bone to the dog, and strain the broth before serving. Per 6-ounce portion, add your chosen booster (lime, chile-garlic, salt; or ginger and turmeric), and drink in bowls or cups immediately.

Greenspan's Grilled Cheese / Tomato-Basil Soup

At the height of summer, when a beautifully lumpy rainbow of heirloom tomatoes is piled high at market, you'll often find a less lovely but still abundant display somewhere off to the side. Unbeautiful seconds, these tomatoes are dented, overripe, and underpriced—perfect for soups and sauces while their *belle laide* sisters get sliced for Instagram-ready platters. Los Angeles's master of tomato soup has got to be Eric Greenspan, whose grilled cheese-devoted eatery is a meditation on the classic combo. Surprisingly nondairy, this puree's robust flavor comes from a lush confit of garlic.

MAKES 2 QUARTS

3 cups olive oil

30 whole garlic cloves, peeled (about 1 cup)

10 ripe tomatoes (roma, heirloom or beefsteak)

1 cup packed basil leaves

2 cups water

1½ tablespoons sriracha

1 tablespoon sugar

1 tablespoon salt

Combine the olive oil and garlic in a medium saucepan. Heat over medium-low heat until bubbles begin to form around the garlic, about 3 minutes. Cook for another 10 minutes. If the garlic begins to brown, lower the heat. Remove from the heat and let cool. Strain the garlic fom the oil.

Meanwhile, core the tomatoes and combine them in a separate large stockpot with the basil, water, sriracha, sugar, and salt. Add 2 cups of the garlic oil and all of the garlic cloves. Stir and bring to a simmer over medium-low heat. Simmer for 45 minutes to 1 hour, until the tomatoes are falling apart.

Working in two batches, transfer the mixture to a blender and puree until smooth, being careful with the hot liquid. Pour into a container and allow to cool to room temperature. To serve, slowly reheat until hot, preferably alongside grilled cheese sandwiches.

Note: This recipe will gift you approximately one extra cup of garlic-infused olive oil from the confit. Sadly, this oil isn't pantry-ready, so serve your fresh bounty alongside the soup with a loaf of crusty country bread and some good dipping balsamic.

Heirloom L.A. / Grilled Pear Gazpacho with Parmesan Cheese Crisps and Red Endive–Walnut Salad

The Eagle Rock-based chefs of Heirloom L.A. and Yolk & Flour–she, Tara Maxey, formerly of Cake Monkey; he, Matthew Poley, formerly of Angelini Osteria–have helped reinvent and reinvigorate the world of high-end catering in L.A., from cooking a la minute and pouring tableside, to sourcing and foraging for local produce and doing their own pasta-making, winemaking, and butchery.

Maxey and Poley know how to work a cocktail hour, and this seductive gazpacho works well when passed as a shooter or topped with a crispy tuile and crunchy red endive-walnut salad as a light first course. It's simple to prepare; and, to serve this vegan soup dairy- or nut-free, just forgo one of the garnishes.

SERVES 4

4 ripe Bartlett pears, peeled, quartered, and cored

Salt and freshly ground black pepper

1 cup olive oil

2 green bell peppers, seeded and diced

1 cup diced peeled white sweet potato

1 cup sweet white wine

¼ cup white balsamic vinegar

Zest and juice of 3 lemons

4 cups water

1 cup basil leaves

TO ASSEMBLE

½ cup grated Parmesan cheese

1 bunch thyme or marjoram leaves

½ cup whole walnuts

1 head red endive, halved

2 tablespoons olive oil

Salt and freshly ground black pepper

To make the soup: Heat a grill to 500°F or heat a cast-iron pan over medium heat for 5 minutes. Toss the pears with salt, pepper, and ½ cup of the olive oil. Grill (or sear) the pears till lightly charred in spots, about 3 minutes per side. Transfer the pears to a plate and set aside.

In a pot, warm ½ cup of the remaining olive oil over medium-high heat until hot but not smoking. Add the bell peppers and sweet potato, reduce the heat to medium, and cook until soft, stirring to make sure they don't brown or sizzle, 6 to 8 minutes. Season with salt and pepper. Add the pears and stir well to incorporate. Carefully pour in the wine, then increase the heat slightly and cook until the liquid has reduced by half. Add the vinegar, lemon zest, juice of 2 lemons, and water. Toss in the basil and simmer for 3 minutes more.

Remove from the heat. Working in two batches, transfer the hot gazpacho to a blender and puree on high until smooth and velvety, being careful with the hot liquid. Taste and adjust the seasoning. Transfer to a clean container and set aside to cool, then cover and chill.

To assemble: Line a plate with paper towels. Place a dry nonstick pan over medium-low heat and sprinkle with enough Parmesan and thyme or marjoram just to cover the bottom of the pan in a thin layer. You are looking for the cheese to melt and toast into a thin, lacy crisp. Use a spatula to loosen the crisp, if necessary, or gently shake the pan, then remove and set aside to cool. Repeat with the remaining cheese and herbs.

In a medium bowl, use your hands to crush the walnuts into large, rustic pieces. Toss with the endive, the remaining lemon juice, 2 tablespoons olive oil, and salt and pepper to taste.

Serve chilled or at room temperature. Ladle the soup into bowls and break off pieces of the Parmesan crisps to float on the surface. Top with the endive-walnut salad.

Croft Alley / Pho Ga (Chicken Pho)

Northern Vietnamese *pho bac* may have a more lively broth, but there's often much more depth to a bowl of southern *pho nam*, owing to that region's agricultural prosperity. At Croft Alley, chef Phuong Tran riffs on that version, replacing the traditional beef with organic chicken broth without sacrificing any of the aromatic comfort. In fact, the broth's infused aromatics are in enormous quantity, especially the star anise, so mind this when shopping. Cassia bark, aka Vietnamese cinnamon, can be found at Southeast Asian markets such as Echo Park's A Grocery Warehouse, which stocks everything from fresh perilla (shiso) to frozen silkworms. If you substitute "regular" cinnamon, Chef Tran suggests cutting the measurement by half.

SERVES 6

1 whole organic chicken

6 liters (about 6 quarts plus 1 cup) water

3 yellow onions, halved crosswise

3 medium thumbs fresh ginger, halved lengthwise

200 grams (7 ounces) star anise pods

200 grams (7 ounces) cassia, or 100 grams (3.5 ounces) cinnamon

100 grams (3½ ounces) fennel seeds

100 grams (3½ ounces) yellow mustard seeds

1 cardamom pod, split

200 grams (7 ounces) rock sugar

Salt

TO ASSEMBLE

1 package rice vermicelli noodles

12 green onions, chopped

24 rings thinly sliced white onion

30 cilantro sprigs

6 heaping handfuls bean sprouts

Thai basil sprigs, parsley, dill or microgreens

12 slices red or green jalapeño

2 limes, quartered

Hoisin sauce (optional)

Sriracha (optional)

Fill an extra-large stockpot with cold water and gently submerge the bird. Bring to a simmer over medium heat.

Meanwhile, heat a large, dry skillet over medium-high heat until almost smoking. Add the onions and ginger and cook without moving until lightly charred and aromatic, 4 to 5 minutes. Flip and lightly char on the other side. Don't stir; the less you fuss with it, the better. Remove the onions and ginger and set aside. In the same skillet, toast the star anise, cassia, fennel seeds, mustard seeds, and cardamom pod, shaking the pan and stirring, until fragrant and lightly colored but not popping or burning, about 1 minute. Remove from the heat to cool, then transfer the spices to a cheesecloth sachet tied with twine.

Once the soup comes to a simmer, skim any foam from the surface and add the charred onions, ginger, and spice sachet. Simmer for 1½ hours. Avoid a full boil, which will make the broth cloudy.

Transfer the chicken to a carving board. When cool enough to handle, break the chicken down into parts and use two forks or fingers to shred the meat into large chunks; let the chicken cool to room temperature. Remove the sachet from the broth and discard. Add the rock sugar and season with salt.

While the chicken is cooling, bring a medium saucepan of water to a boil. Turn off the heat, add the rice noodles to the water, and soak until soft, about 8 minutes, or as directed on the package. Drain.

To assemble: Divide the hot rice noodles among 6 deep bowls and top each with a hefty handful of the chicken. Ladle the broth on top, and sprinkle each equally with the green onions, sliced white onions, and cilantro, and serve with the bean sprouts, Thai basil, jalapeño and lime alongside, with hoisin and sriracha if you like. Serve piping hot.

Orsa & Winston / Red Kuri Squash Soup with Yuzu Koshō Crème Fraîche

Though the soft beauty and polished precision of Josef Centeno's Japanese-Italian crossover tasting menus may seem daunting to tackle at home, this silky autumnal bisque is a great start. Gorgeous red kuri squash grows in sunny areas like California and Florida, and kabocha substitutes nicely. The recipe calls for a few ingredients that require seeking out but are worth it: From the ginger family, grains of paradise contribute a peppery, citrusy pungency; search for them online or in specialty spice markets. Japanese black sugar is an earthy rock candy you can track down in Asian markets, yet unprocessed Asian rock candy or even a spoonful of molasses also works. Definitely find yourself a tube or bottle of yuzu koshō. The magical condiment adds instant acidity, heat, and umami with its eye-opening fermented blend of chiles, citrus, and salt.

SERVES 8

4 tablespoons (½ stick) butter, at room temperature

2 tablespoons smashed Japanese black sugar or rock sugar, or 1 tablespoon molasses

1 teaspoon (3 grams) Diamond Crystal kosher salt

1 teaspoon freshly ground grains of paradise

3 pounds kuri squash (5 or 6 small), halved and seeded

1 cup crème fraîche

1 tablespoon yuzu koshō

4 cups half-and-half (or unsweetened almond milk)

2 teaspoons salt, plus more to taste

Finely chopped chives, for garnish

Togarashi, for garnish

Aonori powder, for garnish

Preheat the oven to 400°F.

In a small bowl, mix the butter with the black sugar, kosher salt, and grains of paradise. Arrange the squash on a rimmed baking sheet, cut-side up. Rub the flesh with the butter mixture and roast until fork-tender, 30 to 45 minutes. Carefully remove from the oven and let cool for at least 10 minutes.

In another bowl, mix the yuzu koshō and crème fraîche until well combined.

Using a spoon, scoop the roasted squash flesh into a large sauce-pan along with any liquid from the baking pan; discard the skins. Add the half-and-half and bring the mixture to a simmer over medium-low heat. Remove from the heat and carefully transfer the mixture to a blender. Puree until smooth. Add 2 teaspoons salt for starters, then taste again and adjust the seasoning as needed.

Ladle 1-cup portions into bowls. Top with 1 tablespoon of the yuzu koshō crème fraîche. Sprinkle with chives and dust with the togarashi and aonori. Serve hot.

Winsome / Charred Escarole Chicken Stew

Winsome sports a peculiar tucked-away feeling, even though its address is Sunset Boulevard. Off Echo Park's main drag, Wendy Haworth's refreshing design reflects the menu's eclecticism. This rustic entry, a charred escarole chicken stew that thickens over time, is a cloudy-day favorite. Nutty farro meets the deep pungency of black garlic, the fruity acid of lime, and the smoky char of grilled escarole.

SERVES 4

1 cup red wheat berries or farro, rinsed thoroughly

Salt

8 cups chicken stock

2 cups chicken broth

1¼ pounds chicken legs or breasts

1 tablespoon extra-virgin olive oil, plus more for the escarole

½ small red onion, thinly sliced

1 teaspoon black garlic paste or minced garlic

¼ cup white wine

4 whole cloves

2 star anise pods

4 whole allspice berries

½ tablespoon fennel seeds

1 head escarole, quartered

Freshly ground black pepper

Juice of 2 limes

Grilled bread, for serving (optional)

Combine the wheat berries or farro with 3 cups water and a large pinch of salt in a saucepan. Bring to a boil, then reduce the heat and simmer, covered, for about 30 minutes, until al dente. Check by tasting for chewiness. If they're not al dente, check every 5 minutes after, possibly up to another 30 minutes (farro will cook faster than wheat berries). Drain.

Combine the chicken stock and broth in a large stockpot. Add the chicken legs and poach over low heat until the legs are cooked but still tender and no longer pink in the center, up to 15 minutes; begin checking the meat at around 8 minutes. A thermometer inserted into the thickest part of the meat (not touching the bone) should register 160 to 165°F. Remove the legs and set aside to cool. Strain the stock and set aside.

In a large pot, warm the olive oil over medium-low heat until hot but not smoking. Add the onion and cook, stirring frequently, until just translucent, about 6 minutes. If you hear sizzling, reduce the heat. Add the black garlic paste and stir to incorporate and toast the paste.

Carefully add the wine, increase the heat to medium-high, and scrape up any browned bits from the bottom of the pan with a wooden spoon. Add the reserved stock and bring back to a boil.

Tie the cloves, star anise, and allspice into a cheesecloth sachet and secure with twine. Once the stew has come to a boil, reduce the heat to low. Add the spice sachet and fennel seeds, cover, and simmer for 20 to 30 minutes. Turn off the heat.

While the stew simmers, use a fork to shred the meat from the chicken, discarding the skin and any small bones and cartilage.

To char the escarole: Heat a grill to medium or heat a cast-iron pan over medium-high heat. Toss the cleaned escarole with olive oil, season with salt and pepper, and place on the grill or in the pan. You want to get some nice char on the escarole, but not let it wilt too much, 2 to 3 minutes. Remove the charred escarole and chop it into 2-inch chunks.

To assemble: Remove the sachet of spices and add the shredded chicken, charred escarole, and farro to the stew. Off the heat, add the lime juice and season with salt. Serve hot, with grilled bread, if you like.

Ricebar / Bisteg Tagalog (Rice Bowl with Soy and Calamansi–Marinated Beef)

Like its well-known cousin adobo, the beefsteak in this Pinoy dish is eaten over rice. So make a bowl out of it, like they do at Charles Olalia and Santos Uy's Ricebar luncheon spot. Their passion is pairing heirloom, non-GMO, Fair Trade rice from the Philippines with hearty recipes. (Here, the recommendation is kalinga unoy rice, a red-freckled grain reminiscent of fired clay.) Cropping up at the farmers' market in winter, the golden or Filipino lime known as calamansi often has a frog-green or orange peel and sunburst insides. Though native to Southeast Asia, the juice is bottled and sold at Asian markets, select Whole Foods Markets, and on Amazon. It's trending, however, so by the time you're reading this, who knows? Kumquat or key lime juice works in a squeeze.

SERVES 4

1½ tablespoons vegetable oil, plus more for searing

1½ teaspoons whole annatto seeds

1 cup soy sauce

1 cup calamansi juice or key lime juice

2½ pounds Angus beef chuck, cut into 2-inch cubes

Diamond Crystal kosher salt and freshly ground black pepper

Dab of butter

2 onions, sliced into ½-inch-thick rounds

Steamed rice, for serving

In a small saucepan, heat the vegetable oil over medium heat until hot but not smoking. Add the annatto seeds. Remove from the heat and set aside for 6 minutes to infuse the oil. Pour the oil through a fine-mesh strainer into a large bowl. Set aside to cool.

Once the oil has cooled, add the soy sauce, calamansi juice, and beef and toss to coat. Cover and marinate in the refrigerator for at least 8 and up to 24 hours.

Remove the meat from the marinade and reserve the liquid. Pat the beef dry and sprinkle with salt and pepper.

Heat a large skillet over medium-high heat and add the oil. Working in batches, sear the beef in the skillet until browned on one side, then turn and sear on a second side until browned, about 2 minutes. Add the butter to the skillet and move the pan to distribute it evenly as it melts. When it begins to smell fragrant, turn the beef and cook until the third and fourth sides are evenly browned as well, another 2 minutes per side. Transfer to a baking dish or roasting pan as you finish each batch.

Pour off and discard all but about 1 tablespoon of the fat in the pan, then return the skillet to medium heat. Add the beef and enough water just to cover, then add the reserved marinade. Bring the mixture to a boil, then reduce the heat to medium-low. Cover and braise for 1 to 1½ hours, until the sauce becomes rich but not too concentrated or dry.

Just before serving, add the onions, cover, raise the heat to bring the sauce to a boil, and boil for 2 minutes. While hot, spoon into bowls over rice.

Lincoln / Farro Bowl with Baby Kale, Smoky Chickpeas, Charred Lemon, and Romesco

A simple, nourishing one-dish supper . . . a stylized take on deconstruction . . . a diplomatic meeting of cross-cultural tastes . . . the humble grain bowl literally and figuratively contains multitudes. Some cooks, like Christine Moore and Pamela Perkins of Lincoln, make the act of content curation look effortless. Note, for example, how the smoke in paprika-spiked chickpeas is echoed not only by the romesco, but also by charred lemon (which is also a great idea to pocket for the oysters on page 145, grilled artichokes, and fish).

SERVES 4

Salt

1 cup farro

1 cup sliced almonds

1 tablespoon canola oil

1 cup drained cooked (or canned) chickpeas

1 tablespoon paprika

1 lemon, cut into quarters

LEMON VINAIGRETTE

¼ cup fresh lemon juice

½ cup olive oil-canola oil blend

Salt and freshly ground black pepper

ROMESCO SAUCE

1 dried pasilla chile

¾ cup roasted red bell peppers (can be jarred)

1 tomato, peeled and seeded

2 garlic cloves, roasted

1 tablespoon sliced almonds

2 tablespoons red wine vinegar

¼ cup plus 1 tablespoon olive oil-canola oil blend

1 teaspoon salt

TO ASSEMBLE

4 cups baby kale

Salt and freshly ground black pepper

Mixed fresh herbs, such as parsley, cilantro, and mint (about ½ cup)

Bring a large pot of salted water to a boil. Add the farro and cook, as if you were making pasta, until the farro has absorbed the liquid and the grain is tender and al dente. Keep tasting it as you go to avoid a chewy result. Use a strainer to transfer the farro to a large bowl and set aside to dry and cool. Discard the cooking liquid.

Meanwhile, preheat the oven to 375°F. Spread the almonds on a rimmed baking sheet and toast in the oven for 8 minutes, or until fragrant and just turning golden. Set aside.

Line a plate with paper towels. In a sauté pan, heat the canola oil over medium heat. When it shimmers, add the chickpeas and paprika and cook for 5 minutes. They will continue to crisp and turn a strong, deep sandy brown. Using a slotted spoon, remove the chickpeas from the pan and drain on the prepared plate. Season with salt and set aside.

Wipe out the pan and set it over high heat until very hot. Place the lemon wedges, flesh-side down, in the pan and char for 5 minutes, then flip and char the second side for 5 minutes. Remove the wedges with tongs and set aside.

To make the lemon vinaigrette: Put the lemon juice in a small bowl. While whisking, very slowly stream in the oil to emulsify. Season with salt and pepper, and set aside.

To make the romesco sauce: Rehydrate the chile by soaking in a bowl of hot water for 10 to 20 minutes, until soft and pliant enough to pat dry, then scrape out the seeds and discard the skin.

Put the chile in a food processor and add the roasted bell peppers, tomato, garlic, and almonds. Process until coarsely ground, pausing to scrape down the sides with a rubber spatula as needed. With the machine running, add the vinegar, then the oil, and salt. (The sauce, which will separate over time, will keep in an airtight container in the refrigerator for 1 to 2 weeks.)

CONTINUED

Farro Bowl, Baby Kale, Smoky Chickpeas, Charred Lemon, Romesco
CONTINUED

To assemble: Add the kale and chickpeas to the bowl with the farro. Toss with ½ cup of the lemon vinaigrette. Season with salt and pepper. Portion the salad into four bowls and garnish each with the toasted almonds, 1 charred lemon wedge, romesco sauce, and herbs.

Patina / Artichoke Velouté

Traditionally, consommés and veloutés display a cook's prowess and mastery of French technique. Patina, now at the exquisite Walt Disney Concert Hall, makes such old-school luxury feel modern, from tableside côte de boeuf carving to a water sommelier. Here, Joachim Splichal teases the essence of spring from humble artichokes in a delicate bisque-style soup. Velouté means "velvet" in French, so you get a hint of its mouthfeel. Artichokes stand up to plenty of seasoning, so don't be shy with the salt and pepper. Make certain to remove all those tough leaves and gristle, or you'll be straining the soup till summer.

SERVES 2

2 to 4 large artichokes (for 2 pounds artichoke hearts)

1 small onion, chopped

1 tablespoon butter, plus more to finish

2 cups chicken broth

¼ cup heavy cream

1 bay leaf

1 sprig thyme

Salt and freshly ground black pepper

Cut the stem off each artichoke and remove the rough outer skin, then slice off the top quarter to remove the sharp leaf tips. Remove the dark outer leaves until left with just the pale, inner leaves near the center. Trim off any dark, rough parts from the base and stem. Cut off the remaining leaves, exposing the heart, and scrape out the choke. If cooking immediately, chop the remaining heart; if not, drop into a bowl of cold water and lemon juice to prevent browning. Repeat with the remaining artichokes.

In a saucepan, melt the butter over medium-high heat. Add the onion and artichoke hearts, and reduce heat to medium-low. Sweat gently until the onions are translucent, about 5 minutes, stirring often—they shouldn't sizzle or brown. Stir in the broth and cream, and add the bay leaf and thyme. Simmer until the artichokes are very tender, 30 to 45 minutes.

When ready, remove and discard the herbs. Transfer to a blender and puree until smooth, working in batches if necessary, being very careful with the hot liquid. Pour the soup through a strainer into a new saucepan and reheat, if necessary. Season with salt, pepper, and additional butter, if desired. Ladle into bowls while hot.

CARB CULTURE

NOODLES, PASTA, AND PIZZA

Crossroads
Sweet Potato Gnocchi with Broccolini Agliolio

Maple Block Meat Co.
Mac & Cheese with Cheddar Crumble

The Butcher's Daughter
Raw Zucchini "Linguine" with Pesto

Felix
Cacio e Pepe

Superba Food + Bread
Bucatini Carbonara

Union
Tagliatelle with Pork Ragù

Chengdu Taste
Sichuan Tan Tan Noodles

Same Same Thai
Chicken Pad See Ew

Love & Salt
Fettuccine with Fennel Sausage, Black Kale, Parmesan, and Bread Crumbs

Bestia
Spaghetti with Sea Urchin

Slow Rise Pizza
High-Hydration Long-Fermented Pan Pizza Dough

Crossroads / Sweet Potato Gnocchi with Broccolini Agliolio

Tal Ronnen of Crossroads has long been a guiding light in elevating plant-based cookery to fine dining status. This eye-catching eggless orange gnocchi showcases California's weeknight favorites, namely sweet potato and Broccolini, while nutritional yeast adds a dash of umami and can be used whenever you'd like the taste of Parmesan without the dairy. Photographer Noah Fecks and food stylist Victoria Granof offer a great tip: Freeze the gnocchi prior to boiling. It'll help maintain their shape. If you don't own a potato ricer, a box grater will mimic the smooth texture of gnocchi. Sure, the results won't be as fine, but isn't a hack better than not making it at all?

SERVES 4 TO 6

**4 large sweet potatoes
(about 2 pounds)**

5 tablespoons extra-virgin olive oil

1½ teaspoons (4 grams) Diamond Crystal kosher salt, plus more as needed

1½ to 2 cups "00" pasta flour (or 3½ to 4 cups for all-purpose flour), plus more for dusting

4 tablespoons (½ stick) Earth Balance butter substitute

1 pound Broccolini or rapini (broccoli rabe)

3 garlic cloves, minced

1 small shallot, minced

1 teaspoon red pepper flakes

Freshly ground black pepper

¼ cup dry sherry

1 cup vegetable stock

2 tablespoons nutritional yeast

¼ cup chopped parsley

Preheat the oven to 400°F. Place the sweet potatoes on a baking sheet. Pierce each several times to allow steam to escape during baking. Roast the sweet potatoes until easily pierced with a fork, 45 minutes to 1 hour.

Remove the sweet potatoes from the oven and while still hot, carefully halve them lengthwise. Scoop out the flesh and transfer to a potato ricer. Rice over a large bowl. Add 1 tablespoon of the olive oil and the salt. Sprinkle in the flour a little at a time, mixing with your hands until a rough dough forms. Take care not to over-work the dough, or it will become tough. Transfer the dough to a lightly floured surface and gently knead for 1 to 2 minutes, until smooth, adding additional flour when necessary to avoid sticking.

Break off a piece of dough and roll it into a rope about index-finger thickness. Cut the rope into 1-inch pieces. Gently roll each down the back of the prongs of a fork while pressing on it with your finger to make a small dimple. The gnocchi should be bullet-sized, slightly curved, and marked with ridges to "trap" sauce. Put the gnocchi in a single layer on a flour-dusted baking sheet. Cover with plastic wrap. Repeat with the remaining dough, then freeze the sheet of gnocchi for at least 30 minutes.

In a large sauté pan, heat the remaining 4 tablespoons olive oil and the butter substitute over medium-high heat. When the butter substitute has melted, add the Broccolini or rapini, garlic, and shallot. Cook, stirring, until fragrant and softened, about 2 minutes. Season with the red pepper flakes and salt and black pepper to taste.

Carefully add the sherry and cook until the liquid has nearly evap-orated, about 30 seconds. Stir in the stock. Simmer for 4 minutes, then reduce the heat to medium-low. Sprinkle in the nutritional yeast and parsley and cook until the sauce thickens slightly, about 5 minutes. Taste and adjust the seasoning. Cover and keep warm.

Meanwhile, bring a large pot of salted water to a boil. Without overcrowding, add the gnocchi in batches and cook until they float to the surface, 2 to 4 minutes. Use a strainer or slotted spoon to lift and drain well. Place the gnocchi in the pan to gently toss to coat in sauce. Transfer to a serving platter. Serve while hot.

Maple Block Meat Co. / Mac & Cheese with Cheddar Crumble

Should you find yourself driving down a certain stretch of Sepulveda in Culver City, roll down the windows and take in the glorious perfume of peach and applewood-burning barbecue from Maple Block Meat Co. Indeed, once chef Adam Cole burst onto the L.A. scene, even Texan food writers had to admit, this might be some of the best barbecue out West. Cole's crunchy, gooey macaroni and cheese sidekicks all the sweet and spice, but in our book it's a star. If pressed for time, Cole recommends skipping the crumble and crushing cheese crackers on top.

SERVES 4 TO 6

CHEDDAR CRUMBLE
1 pound sharp cheddar cheese, grated
½ cup (1 stick) butter, at room temperature
1½ cups all-purpose flour
1 teaspoon (3 grams) Diamond Crystal kosher salt
¼ teaspoon cayenne

MAC & CHEESE
3 tablespoons butter
¼ cup vegetable oil
2 pounds yellow onions, sliced ¼-inch thick
¼ cup all-purpose flour
4 cups milk
1 tablespoon (9 grams) Diamond Crystal kosher salt
1 teaspoon freshly ground black pepper
1 teaspoon paprika
½ teaspoon mustard powder
½ nutmeg, grated
1½ pounds white American cheese, grated
1 pound elbow macaroni
Chopped chives, for garnish

To make the cheddar crumble: Preheat the oven to 400°F.

In the bowl of a stand mixer fitted with the paddle attachment, combine the cheese, butter, flour, salt, and cayenne. Mix on low speed until a dough forms. Divide the dough into four pieces. Put one piece between two sheets of parchment paper and roll it out as thin as possible (about ¼-inch thick). Repeat with the remaining pieces of dough. Place these on a baking sheet and bake for 7 minutes, then rotate and bake for 6 to 8 minutes more, until the dough is golden brown. Remove from the oven and let cool on the pan to room temperature. Crumble by hand or in a food processor. (The cheddar crumble will keep in an airtight container at room temperature for up to 1 week.)

To make the macaroni and cheese: In a medium or large pot, melt the butter with the vegetable oil over medium-low heat. Add the onions, cover, and sweat them, stirring to avoid browning, until translucent and tender, about 6 minutes. If you hear sizzling, reduce the heat. Continue cooking the onions over low heat until they are very tender and falling apart, 30 to 45 minutes more. Add the flour, stirring continuously with a whisk or wooden spoon to prevent sticking as the sauce thickens. After 5 minutes, raise the heat to medium-high and whisk in the milk. Bring the mixture to a full simmer and cook until very well thickened, about 10 minutes more (while stirring, keep scraping the bottom of the pot to prevent scorching).

Carefully transfer the mixture to a blender and puree until smooth. Return the sauce to the pot over low heat. Add the salt, pepper, paprika, mustard powder, and nutmeg and whisk to fully incorporate. Whisk in small amounts of grated cheese at a time to melt. Once incorporated, keep warm on the stove.

To assemble: Bring an aggressively salted pot of water to a boil. Add the macaroni and cook until al dente. Drain the pasta and return it to the pot. Using equal amounts of pasta and cheese sauce, combine the two over medium heat, stirring to fully incorporate. Add more sauce, if needed, to reach the desired consistency. Transfer to a serving dish and top with the cheddar crumble and chives.

The Butcher's Daughter / Raw Zucchini "Linguine" with Pesto

Green, creamy, a little goddess-y, this refreshing vegan and gluten-free summer "nah-sta" pesto by executive chef Richard Rea at New York export Butcher's Daughter in Venice is as zeitgeist-y as it gets. It's crafted using a spiralizer–a gratifying, inexpensive tool with deceptively sharp teeth and holes. Serving the extra pesto on the side with the almond meal helps with the texture, while nutritional yeast gives a little boost of cheese flavor. Of course, heathens seeking to undo all this plant-based goodness can add strips of grilled flank steak to the finished dish.

SERVES 4

8 medium zucchini, ends trimmed

1 cup raw walnuts

½ cup almond meal

Zest of 1 lemon

3 tablespoons fresh lemon juice

1½ cups olive oil

2 teaspoons sea salt, plus more as needed

2 bunches fresh basil

Cherry tomatoes, halved (optional)

Nutritional yeast, for garnish (optional)

Using a spiralizer fitted with the small julienne attachment, cut the zucchini into noodles. Instead of endlessly long strands, they'll be easier to eat if you cut the noodles to the length of regular pasta.

In a blender, combine the walnuts, ¼ cup of the almond meal, the lemon zest, lemon juice, olive oil, and salt and puree until smooth. Stop the blender and scrape down the sides. Add the basil and blend until fully incorporated. Season very well.

To assemble: Put the zucchini noodles a large serving bowl, and dust with the remaining ¼ cup almond meal. Add enough pesto to coat the noodles without drenching them, and serve any extra on the side. Serve at room temperature with cherry tomatoes and nutritional yeast, if desired.

Felix / Cacio e Pepe

How can cheese and pepper be transcendent? Felix chef and partner Evan Funke can tell you. Though he certainly honors the Italian canon in particular, he doesn't blindly accept dogmatic rules around the craft. "Authenticity is a very personal thing," he says, "but tradition breeds bad habits, too."

"*Cacio e pepe* has its roots in an indefinite past that borders on myth," he says. "Depending on whose grandmother you are talking to, its story likely contains widespread variation. Its origins trace to the Roman Campagna and into the mountains of Abruzzo and Umbria, where shepherds packed foods that could not only withstand extended periods of time in the countryside but were also delicious, warming, and nutritious. In this case: dried pasta, salted sheep's-milk cheese, and black pepper. Though this recipe may not be 'traditional' according to some opinions, its authenticity is rooted in my own personal experiences in Lazio, Umbria, and Abruzzo."

SERVES 2

Salt

9 ounces fresh or dried spaghetti, bucatini, or rigatoni

1 tablespoon butter

Black peppercorns (loaded into a pepper mill)

Pecorino Romano, for grating

Set oven-safe plates in the oven at its lowest setting. Alternatively, rinse the plates in very hot water just before serving, towel dry, and keep them wrapped in a dishtowel.

Bring water to a rolling boil in a heavy-bottomed pot. Salt the water as if it were an aggressively seasoned soup, but not so much like the ocean. Add your pasta to the water, allow it to relax, then give it a stir. Throughout the cooking process, test the doneness of the pasta. You are looking for a crunchy al dente.

While the pasta cooks, grind 50 turns from the peppermill. (Funke prefers a mix of finely ground and coarsely ground black pepper.) In a 10-inch sauté pan, toast the pepper over low heat until its aromatics release, about 1 minute. Be careful not to burn the pepper: If it smokes, your pan is too hot. Raise the heat to medium and quickly add the butter. As it melts, fry the pepper in the frothy butter for about 30 seconds, but do not brown the butter—it will alter the taste of the finished sauce.

Add a 6-ounce (¾-cup) ladle of the pasta water to the skillet and whisk to emulsify the sauce. Bring to a boil, then reduce the heat to medium-low. With tongs, transfer the pasta from the water to the sauce. Toss vigorously until the sauce coats the pasta. If it seems dry, add another half ladle (6 tablespoons) of the pasta water until the sauce comes together. Taste and adjust the seasoning, if needed (pecorino is highly seasoned already, so keep this in mind).

Transfer the pasta to the warmed plates. Spoon any excess sauce on top. Liberally grate cheese over the top of the pasta. Finish with a few last turns of pepper and serve immediately.

Superba Food + **Bread** / Bucatini Carbonara

For tucking into bowls of all kinds, Superba Food + Bread is breezy Venice's most golden-lit, open-air setting. To recreate that feeling at home, toasting readymade dried pasta is our adaptation of Superba's smoked flour and can be prepped ahead of time. (Note that liquid smoke has a way of infusing everything from the water to your hair to your clothes, so add it to the pasta water seconds before you cook the bucatini.) Also: The final step of grating in the Parmesan marks the point of no return, so have your bowls preheated, table set, and candles lit.

SERVES 4

1 pound bucatini

3 tablespoons salt, plus more as needed

2 tablespoons liquid smoke

1 pound bacon (not applewood-smoked)

4 cups water

¼ cup white vinegar

4 large eggs

2 tablespoons coarsely ground black pepper, plus more to garnish

½ cup heavy cream

1¼ cups mascarpone cheese

½ cup finely grated Parmesan cheese, plus more to garnish

Preheat the oven to 500°F. On a baking sheet, spread the pasta flat. Bake for 5 to 7 minutes, until strongly toasted and browned. Very carefully slide the pasta onto a rack to cool. Reduce the oven temperature to 350°F.

In a large pot, bring about 4 quarts of water to a rolling boil. Aggressively salt the water, add the liquid smoke, then the pasta. Cook until al dente, checking for doneness throughout, about 11 minutes. Strain the pasta, reserving the pasta water.

While the pasta is cooking, line a rack with paper towels. On a rimmed baking sheet, layer the bacon flat so the pieces don't overlap. Bake until crispy and the fat has rendered, 12 to 18 minutes, depending on the thickness. Remove from the oven, being mindful of the grease, and transfer the bacon to the lined rack. Once cooled, chop finely and set aside ¼ cup for garnish.

Poach the eggs individually: In a small saucepan fitted with a thermometer, combine the water, vinegar, and salt. Over medium heat, bring the water to 180°F. (Bubbles should form on the side of the pan.) Crack an egg into a coffee cup or ramekin. Using a slotted spoon, swirl the water in the saucepan as you gently drop in the egg–this action helps the wispy egg whites wrap around the yolk. Poach for 3 minutes. Using a slotted spoon, carefully transfer the egg to a paper towel or plastic wrap–lined plate. Repeat with the remaining eggs, keeping the water temperature steady.

To assemble: Preheat your bowls. In a 12-inch sauté pan, toast the black pepper over medium heat. As the pepper begins to smoke, add the bacon and stir with a wooden spoon. Slowly pour in the cream. As the liquid begins to simmer, reduce the heat to medium-low and stir. Scrape up the browned bits from the bottom of the pan. Once the froth has died down and the color evens out, whisk in the mascarpone until smooth. Raise the heat slightly, add the pasta to the pan, and toss. It should take about 1 minute to come together. Add the cheese, and toss again. Transfer the pasta to bowls and garnish each with a poached egg, the reserved chopped bacon, and a crack of black pepper.

Union / Tagliatelle with Pork Ragù

Master of a canon that includes hearty pastas, porchetta, sausages, and spice blends, Bruce Kalman turns California's divine ingredients into regional Italian classics at Union in Pasadena and Grand Central's Knead & Co pasta bar.

Instead of simmering on the stove, this ragù goes into the oven, maximizing the browning of the sauce when uncovered in its final minutes of cooking. This has less to do with color than with umami. Before hesitating on the pig trotters or ham hocks, note that bones are what contribute the gelatin to transform the sauce from watery to rich and thick. Union gussies up this ragù with gremolata, an Italian confetti of minced garlic, lemon zest, and parsley for roasted meats. Its crisp jolt is worth the knife time. Making your own tagliatelle is surprisingly easy, but any dried broad noodle will work.

SERVES 6, WITH EXTRA RAGÙ TO FREEZE

TAGLIATELLE

1 pound semolina (durum) flour, plus more for dusting

14 ounces egg yolks (18 to 20 large eggs)

PORK RAGÙ

½ cup olive oil, plus more as needed

2 tablespoons chopped fresh oregano

2 tablespoons chopped fresh sage

2 tablespoons chopped fresh rosemary

4 ounces guanciale or smoked bacon, cut into lardons

2 pounds ground pork

10 garlic cloves, smashed

2 teaspoons red pepper flakes

1 cup finely diced yellow onion

½ cup finely diced celery

½ cup finely diced fennel bulb

½ cup finely diced carrots

2 bay leaves

1 (750-ml) bottle dry red wine

2 quarts (64 ounces) San Marzano tomatoes, passed through the large holes of a food mill or crushed by hand

2 quarts (64 ounces) chicken broth

2 pig's trotters or smoked ham hocks, wrapped in cheesecloth

To make the tagliatelle: In the bowl of a stand mixer fitted with the dough hook, begin mixing the flour on medium speed. Slowly add the egg yolks and mix for about 5 minutes, until the dough forms a ball, then begins to pull away from the sides of the bowl, then the bottom of the bowl. If the ball of dough does not form, add small amounts of water at a time until you reach this consistency. Transfer the dough to a wooden cutting board and knead until the dough is fairly smooth and firm, about 5 minutes. Wrap with plastic wrap and refrigerate for at least 6 hours.

Return the dough to the cutting board. Using a rolling pin, roll the dough thin enough to fit into a pasta machine roller. On the widest setting, begin passing the dough through the roller into a sheet and repeat until the dough is smooth and silky. Adjust the roller to a thinner setting and continue until the dough is thin, not chunky. Cut the sheet into 12-inch lengths. Using a tagliatelle cutter attachment, cut the pasta sheets into noodles. Toss with semolina to avoid sticking and place on a baking sheet.

To make the ragù: Preheat the oven to 250°F.

In a large pot or Dutch oven, warm the olive oil over medium heat until hot but not smoking. Add the herbs and cook, stirring, until fragrant and crispy, then carefully remove the herbs and set aside. Add the guanciale to the oil and cook, stirring well, until cooked through. Add the ground pork, breaking up the meat with a wooden spoon. Season with salt and pepper and cook until slightly browned. Clear a space in the center of the pot, add a little more oil, then add the garlic and red pepper flakes. Cook for 3 minutes, stirring occasionally to avoid burning. Add the onion, celery, fennel, carrots, and bay leaves and season again, then stir the vegetables and pork together. Add the wine, bring to a

CONTINUED

Tagliatelle with Pork Ragù
CONTINUED

2 tablespoons butter

6 basil leaves

TO ASSEMBLE

½ cup grated Parmesan, plus more for garnish

2 tablespoons extra-virgin olive oil, plus more for garnish

simmer, then reduce the heat and cook till the liquid reduces by half, about 15 minutes. Add the tomatoes, broth, trotters, and the fried herbs.

Cover and transfer the pot to the oven. Cook, stirring occasionally, 2 to 3 hours, until the liquid is reduced and the ragù is thick. At the end of the cook time, remove the cover and allow the top to brown for 10 minutes. Carefully remove the pot from the oven. Skim off the top layer of fat.

Fill a large saucepan a little more than halfway with water. Bring to a boil and salt aggressively.

In a large saucepan, heat 3 cups of the ragù over medium heat. (Allow the remainder to cool a bit before portioning it to freeze in airtight containers or freezer bags.) Add the butter and basil leaves, stirring, until the butter is incorporated. Taste and adjust the seasoning. Keep the finished ragù warm while cooking the pasta.

Once the water boils, add the tagliatelle and cook until al dente, 2 to 3 minutes. Make sure to stir immediately after dropping in the pasta, or it will tangle and stick.

Using a slotted spoon or strainer, transfer the cooked pasta directly to the ragù and toss to combine. Add a ladle of pasta cooking water if the sauce is too thick. Stir the pasta in the sauce over low heat for 2 minutes. Add the Parmesan and olive oil and toss well. Check the seasoning, then transfer the pasta to a serving bowl and garnish with additional Parmesan and olive oil. Serve immediately.

FARMERS MARKET Schedule

MON: west hollywood

TUES: pasadena & silver lake

WED: santa monica & pasadena

THUR: South Pasadena & DTLA @ 7th & Fi

FRI: eagle rock & echo par

SAT: pasadena & silver la

SUN: old Hollywo & own Pasade

Chengdu Taste / Sichuan Tan Tan Noodles

In Sichuan, chile oil signifies generosity. Here in San Gabriel Valley, Tony Xu's *tan tan* noodles at Chengdu Taste tempt locals, tourists, and every type of noodle-loving Angeleno with their generous tangle of flavors and textures. With this classic, the fermented vegetables may differ on occasion, yet the constant is the Sichuan peppercorn. Its particular effect is a numbing, tingling paresthesia in the mouth and lips—a tiny, invigorating nerve shock—accompanying the lightly tart and spicy floral aromatics of a dried berry that's neither pepper nor chile.

Seek out Asian sesame paste as opposed to tahini; the former toasts the seeds, while the latter uses raw.

SERVES 2

2 teaspoons peanut oil

5½ ounces minced or ground pork

Salt

¼ cup preserved mustard greens (*suì mǐ yá cài*)

1 tablespoon shaoxing wine (or dry sherry)

2 tablespoons soy sauce

1½ teaspoons whole Sichuan peppercorns, lightly smashed

2 tablespoons chile oil

2½ teaspoons sugar

1 tablespoon Asian-style sesame paste

12 ounces fresh or dried white Sichuan-style noodles, medium thickness

1 green onion, chopped

Sesame seeds, for garnish

Chopped peanuts, for garnish

In a large skillet or wok, warm the peanut oil over medium-high heat until just smoking. Add the pork and a pinch of salt. Cook until browned, with almost no traces of prink. Add the preserved mustard greens and stir. The pork will begin to darken and become crisp. Pour in the shaoxing wine and 1 tablespoon of the soy sauce, and cook until the liquid has evaporated. Set aside.

In a small bowl, stir together the remaining 1 tablespoon soy sauce, the Sichuan peppercorns, chile oil, sugar, and sesame paste. The consistency should be like a thin gravy—just thick enough to coat the back of a spoon and hold a line when you draw your finger through it. Divide the sauce between two soup or pasta bowls.

Bring a large pot of water to a boil. Add the noodles and cook according to the package instructions (usually 4 to 5 minutes), till tender but still al dente. Reserve 2 cups of the cooking water. Drain and rinse the noodles with cold water, and divide between the bowls.

To assemble: Top the noodles with the pork mixture and green onion. Garnish with sesame seeds and peanuts. Serve at room temperature. Mix thoroughly before eating. (If the sauce is too tight, add a bit of the reserved pasta water.)

Same Same Thai / Chicken Pad See Ew

The owners of Rambutan Thai may have handed over the running of the business, but to let everybody know, they renamed it with a wink. This wok-fried noodle favorite from their kitchen also comes together in a blink, so have all your ingredients handy. What's so lovely about Thai cuisine is the protein modularity, and while we've gone with chicken, you could easily sub in flank steak, tofu, or whatever's on hand.

The caramel-savory of sweet dark soy sauce has legs—enough to coat the noodles, anyway. Indonesians use a variant called *kecap manis*, in case you come across it. Should the dark kind elude you, 3 tablespoons regular soy sauce plus ½ to 1 tablespoon brown sugar or molasses will lend some body. If you have any problems with sticking while you stir-fry, add a little more oil.

SERVES 2

8 ounces Chinese broccoli, stalks and leaves

1 tablespoon canola oil

1 egg

2 garlic cloves, minced

6 ounces boneless, skinless chicken thighs or breasts, sliced into bite-size pieces

8 ounces fresh wide rice stick noodles, separated

1 teaspoon salted soybean paste

2 tablespoons sweet dark soy sauce

1 tablespoon regular soy sauce

2 teaspoons distilled white vinegar

½ teaspoon sugar

Freshly ground white and black pepper

Fish sauce, for garnish (optional)

Red chile powder, for garnish (optional)

Vinegar with pickled chile, for garnish (optional)

Separate the leaves from the broccoli stalks, and slice the stalks into thin sticks. Set aside.

In a wok, heat the canola oil over high heat until almost smoking. Crack the egg into the oil, then quickly add the garlic. Using a wooden spoon, stir until the egg is starting to form curds, about 30 seconds. Add the chicken and Chinese broccoli and stir-fry until the chicken is just cooked through, about 2 minutes.

Add the rice noodles, soybean paste, sweet soy sauce, regular soy sauce, vinegar, and sugar. Stir-fry until the noodles soften and absorb most of the sauce, about 1 minute. You want the sauce to coat the noodles evenly, until caramelized. If you like your noodles just a bit crispy, keep the noodles touching the hot bottom of the pan.

To assemble: Remove from the heat and transfer to a serving platter. Dust with white and black pepper and serve immediately with fish sauce, red chile powder, and pickled chile as garnish, if desired.

Love & Salt / Fettuccine with Fennel Sausage, Black Kale, Parmesan, and Bread Crumbs

Manhattan Beach has proven itself both postcard-perfect and a surprising dining destination. At chef Michael Fiorelli's Love & Salt, you're falling in love with fired-up pizza, kale salads, and killer pastas like this fennel sausage number. For four, you need about half the sausage in the recipe, so freeze the remainder in an airtight container. Take a chance on California-harvested fennel pollen; its intensity is worth the expense.

SERVES 4

FENNEL SAUSAGE

2 tablespoons fennel seeds

2½ tablespoons finely minced garlic

1½ teaspoons (4½ grams) Diamond Crystal kosher salt

¼ teaspoon red pepper flakes

½ teaspoon freshly ground black pepper

1½ teaspoons hot paprika

1½ teaspoons sugar

1 pound ground pork

¼ pound pork fat (not lard), diced

2 tablespoons red wine vinegar

Ice water

TO ASSEMBLE

1 loaf day-old bread, such as ciabatta, cut into ½-inch cubes

Olive oil

Salt and freshly ground black pepper

8 ounces dried fettuccine

2 cups chicken stock

4 tablespoons (½ stick) butter

¼ cup grated Parmesan, plus more for garnish (or nutritional yeast)

3 tablespoons finely chopped parsley

1 teaspoon fennel pollen, plus more for garnish (optional)

1 teaspoon (3 grams) Diamond Crystal kosher salt, plus more as needed

1 teaspoon red pepper flakes

2 bunches Tuscan black kale, stemmed, leaves torn into 1-inch pieces

To make the sausage: Heat a small skillet over medium heat. Add the fennel seeds and toast until fragrant—don't let them burn. Let cool, then grind in a molcajete or spice grinder.

Transfer the fennel to a large bowl and add the garlic, salt, red pepper flakes, black pepper, paprika, and sugar. Stir to incorporate. Add the ground pork and fatback. Toss to coat, cover, and refrigerate for 24 hours or freeze until very cold. Chill the bowl of a stand mixer overnight.

The next day, chill the vinegar and set up the mixer with the grinder attachment. Set the chilled mixer bowl over a bowl of ice. Pass the sausage mixture through the grinder into the mixer bowl. Working efficiently (to keep the meat as cold as possible), replace the grinder with the paddle attachment. Mix on low speed, gradually adding the chilled vinegar and ¼ cup ice water until well combined and slightly sticky.

To assemble: Preheat the oven to 325°F.

In a large bowl, toss the bread cubes with just enough oil to lightly coat. Season with salt and black pepper. Transfer to a baking sheet and bake for 15 minutes, or just until golden brown. Let the bread cool, then transfer to a food processor and pulse to a rustic crumb. Set aside.

Bring a pot of aggressively salted water to a boil. Add the fettuccine and cook for 1 minute less than directed on the package. (The pasta will finish cooking in the sauce.) Drain well and set aside.

In a large heavy-bottomed sauté pan, heat 2 tablespoons olive oil over medium-high heat until hot but not smoking. Add half the fennel sausage and cook, breaking up the meat with a wooden spoon, until golden brown, about 3 minutes. Pour in the stock and bring to a boil, scraping the bottom of the pan with a wooden spoon. Reduce the heat slightly and add the butter, Parmesan, 3 tablespoons of the bread crumbs, the parsley, fennel pollen (if using), kosher salt, and red pepper flakes. Bring to a simmer, and

CONTINUED

allow the liquid to reduce slightly, until the butter has melted and the mixture has thickened.

Using tongs, add the cooked pasta to the sauce, then top with the kale and cook just to wilt. Lightly simmer the pasta for 1 final minute while tossing, then transfer to warmed plates. Garnish each serving with Parmesan, the remaining bread crumbs, and a pinch of fennel pollen, if using. Serve immediately.

Bestia / Spaghetti with Sea Urchin

It is a luxury to take the time to treat oneself. That's why the measurements for this over-the-top pasta are listed for one (hungry) person—or two for date night. You can scale it up, but sometimes it's nice to hang solo with a glass of German Riesling, an old novel you've been meaning to finish, and a new bowl of pasta that you definitely will.

Bestia's signature spaghetti rustichella, adapted and super-streamlined here, never seems to disappear from the menu. Chef Ori Menashe makes Calabrian chile and even squid ink bottarga in house; the rest of us can find all these specialty products at local Italian markets. Depending on your appreciation for spiky sea urchin (uni), start small and calibrate how much or little you'd like to blend in. For those who haven't yet acquired the taste, nix the urchin and pile on lobster.

SERVES 1 OR 2

Diamond Crystal kosher salt

4 ounces dry spaghetti

¼ cup extra-virgin olive oil, plus more for garnish

1 heaping tablespoon chopped shallot

1 teaspoon chopped garlic

1 teaspoon chopped Calabrian chile

½ teaspoon salt

¼ cup white wine

6 tablespoons lobster stock

¾ cup vegetable stock, plus more as needed

1 to 5 fresh uni lobes, plus 1 per plate for garnish

Bottarga, for grating

2 Thai basil leaves, thinly sliced

1 teaspoon chopped flat-leaf parsley

Fresh lemon juice, for garnish

Sea salt, for garnish

Bring a large pot of water to a boil. Season it aggressively with salt. Add the spaghetti and cook for about 6 minutes.

Meanwhile, in a saucepan, heat the olive oil over low heat. Add the shallot, garlic, chile, and ½ teaspoon salt. Gently and slowly sweat the vegetables, stirring often, until translucent. If you hear sizzling, reduce the heat. Carefully add the wine, then increase the heat to medium, and bring to a boil, using a wooden spoon to scrape up any browned bits from the pan. Cook, stirring, until the liquid has almost completely evaporated. Pour in the lobster stock and cook to reduce and thicken. Add the vegetable stock to the pan.

After 6 minutes, quickly drain the pasta and add to the saucepan. Toss the pasta in the stock mixture to help the sauce come together, adding more vegetable stock, if necessary. Once the sauce is thick and the pasta is al dente, remove from the heat.

In a bowl, use a rubber spatula to smash and smooth the texture of all but one uni. Add the pasta and toss to combine the sauce and uni. Adjust the seasoning, then transfer to a serving bowl or plates. To garnish, grate bottarga over the bowl and sprinkle with basil and parsley. Garnish with the final piece of uni on top, seasoned with 2 drops of lemon juice, a sprinkle of sea salt, and a drizzle of oil. Serve while hot.

Slow Rise Pizza / High-Hydration Long-Fermented Pizza Dough

Ever wonder whom the chefs behind Bestia, Republique, Rose Café, and other kitchens across L.A. call for help juggling the times, temperatures, and fermentation schedules involved in making pizza dough? Noel Brohner of Slow Rise Pizza, freelance pizzaiolo.

While much glory goes to blistery, thin Neapolitan-style crust, the heat and skillset required to make them doesn't adapt easily to home ovens. Instead, Brohner's specially developed recipe offers success: pro-quality, light and airy, thick-crusted Roman-style pizza. The specialty equipment needed is a stand mixer, pizza stone, and two Cambros or food-safe lidded containers. Once you get the hang of mixing dough and fermenting in the fridge, dough is like having half a bottle of wine in the fridge and knowing what to do with it other than drinking it. This dinner party-friendly recipe makes enough dough for two 1,200-gram or four 600-gram pan pizzas. The possibilities, however, are endless; for example, you can pull portions off during the week and transform them into pizza breads, Pullman loaves, or weekend French toast.

MAKES ONE BATCH OF 2440 GRAMS DOUGH

DOUGH

1,300 grams (46 ounces, or 100% baker's percentage) King Arthur "Special" Bread Flour

1,105 grams (39 ounces, or 85% baker's percentage) filtered or mineral water

31 grams (1 ounce, or 2.4% baker's percentage) Diamond Crystal kosher salt

5 grams (.2 ounce, or .4% baker's percentage) instant dry yeast

Olive oil, for the container

To mix the dough: Several hours ahead of mixing, place a clean stand mixer bowl in the freezer. Using a digital scale, weigh out the flour, water, salt, and yeast separately and set aside. Put the water in the refrigerator till 40°F or colder. (In particularly hot climates or kitchens, you might reduce the measurement of instant dry yeast to 4 grams and chill the flour, too.)

Remove the mixer bowl from the freezer and add the water first, then the flour. Attach the bowl to the stand mixer and fit the mixer with the dough hook. Set out a stopwatch. Lock the mixer head and turn the mixer to 1 or very low speed (numbered speeds below are based on a KitchenAid stand mixer). Start the stopwatch.

At 1 minute, pause the stopwatch and mixer. Scrape down the sides of the bowl with a rubber spatula or dough scraper. Restart the stopwatch and the mixer on the same speed.
At 2 minutes, raise the speed to 2.
At 3 minutes, raise to 3.
At 4 minutes, raise to 4.
At 5 minutes, raise to 5.
At 6 minutes, raise to 6.
At 7 minutes, reduce the mixer speed back to 1, and without stopping the motor, add the yeast.
At 8 minutes, add the salt, still at speed 1.
At 9 minutes, raise the mixer speed back to 6. After a few additional minutes, the dough should begin to make slapping sounds as the gluten develops. The dough will slowly begin to climb up the dough hook.
At 16 to 18 minutes, the dough should begin to pull away from the sides of the bowl.

CONTINUED

High-Hydration Long-Fermented Pizza Dough

At 18 to 20 minutes, the dough should pull away from the sides of the bowl completely.

At around 20 minutes, the texture of the dough should begin to smooth out. When the dough ball completely pulls away from the bottom of the bowl, mix for 1 minute more. (Some flours simply take longer, so if you find yours doesn't ball up as indicated above, you may simply need to wait a little longer, up to 25 to 30 minutes, while it mixes. While it's too late to add flour at this stage, you can take the bowl off the mixer and let it rest, covered with a towel, in the refrigerator or freezer for up to 30 minutes. The flour has additional time to absorb the water and the reduction in temperature will slightly firm up the dough. Next time, reduce the amount of water, and vice versa.) Reduce the mixer speed slowly from speed 6 to speed 1, then stop the mixer.

A window-pane test on a small piece of dough will help check for gluten development before moving onto bulk fermentation: Wet your hands, tear off a small piece, and spread it between two fingers on each hand to see if it will stretch without breaking. If it breaks, the gluten has not developed and needs to rest more. The dough should stretch well and be translucent.

For the bulk fermentation: Apply a thin coating of olive oil to the inside surface of a 6-quart Cambro, food-safe plastic container, or a bucket with a non-airtight cover large enough to allow the dough to double or triple in size. Using a dough scraper, transfer the dough into the container, cover with a non-airtight lid, and refrigerate for 30 minutes. The dough needs to "breathe" as it converts sugars into CO_2, but you don't want cold refrigerator air to dry out its surface; covering the dough with a kitchen towel will work here, but not for the longer rest later, so a container with a non-airtight lid (such as a Cambro half–hotel pan) is your best bet.

After 30 minutes, remove the dough from the refrigerator. Stretching and folding the dough in the container while it chills helps it cool evenly and helps add structure to the final dough. Place the container on a work surface. Reach just underneath one side of the dough along and pull straight up from the bottom, so it stretches, and fold up into the center of the container, as if folding a blanket in a box. Repeat this on all four sides to complete one full set of stretch-and-folds. Chill the container, covered, for another 30 minutes (set your timer), then repeat on each side. After another full set of stretch-and-folds, return the dough, covered, to the refrigerator.

After these two sets of stretch and folds, the dough will be ready for use in as little as 24 hours but will keep for up to 5

days. Place it toward the back of the fridge, where opening and closing won't affect the temperature. As it continues to ferment in the refrigerator, it will develop in flavor and complexity. Open the container daily to check fermentation for air bubbles, sweet aroma, and consistent rise.

To divide the dough and preshape (secondary fermentation): On the morning of the day you plan to bake, remove the dough container from the refrigerator and allow it to sit for 1 to 2 hours at room temperature. Use a dough scraper to carefully scrape the sides of the container to loosen the dough. Gently turn the container upside-down just above a clean, dry work surface generously dusted with flour and let gravity release the dough in one even piece.

Flour your hands and fold the dough ball in half by bringing the edge farthest from you to meet the closest, enclosing the unfloured top side. Using the palms of your hands, gently pat out the dough to an even thickness. Using a bench knife, divide the dough into two even pieces (about 1,200 grams each). Quickly form each piece of dough into a tight, round ball (as much as you can; the dough will be wetter than bread dough), keeping the raw flour on the outside from getting into the inside during shaping. If the dough sticks, use more flour on your hands and work surface.

Lightly oil two plastic containers or wide bowls and place each ball, seam-side up, into each and cover. Depending on the room temperature, the balls should be allowed to rise for 4 to 6 hours, or up to 8 hours if the weather is cold.

To shape and bake the dough: Preheat the oven to 500°F with a pizza stone on the lowest rack. (If your oven maxes out below 500°F, don't fear, you'll get the same results, but your cooking time may increase 5 to 10 minutes.) Very generously coat a baking sheet with olive oil. Once one dough ball has doubled or tripled in size, turn its container upside-down just above the baking sheet, releasing the dough slowly and gently in one even piece.

Generously oil the top of the dough ball. Using spread fingertips with a dimpling motion, spread the dough out across the pan in an even thickness. Be gentle so as not to deflate the dough. If the dough is being stubborn, let it rest for a few minutes at room temperature before continuing.

CONTINUED

High-Hydration Long-Fermented Pizza Dough
CONTINUED

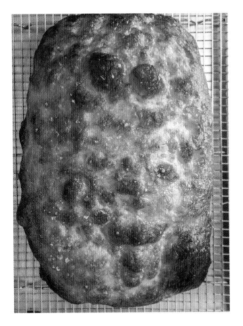

Lightly but evenly top the dough with your choice of toppings (see sidebar) and press gently with flat palms.

Place the pan directly on top of the pizza stone and bake for 20 to 25 minutes, rotating the pizza once. After about 18 minutes, use a thin metal spatula to lift the dough just off the sides and bottom of the pan, and check for doneness. If the bottom is cooking faster than the top, place the pan on an oven rack (not on the pizza stone) for the remainder of the bake. If not, return the pan to the pizza stone to finish. Add any toppings that require little baking time.

When the pizza is baked, remove the pan from the oven. Allow to cool for a moment, then use a spatula to carefully remove the whole pizza from the baking sheet, and transfer to a wire rack. One of the pizza facts of life is that sometimes it sticks a bit, especially if your toppings have dripped over the side, but what allows it to release easily is being cooked well. If there's an unnecessary amount of struggle with the pan, the pizza is likely undercooked or not hot or crisp enough. Another 2 to 3 minutes on the stone will have the bottom crust crunching like chips! (For the next pizza, you can try a non-stick spray in addition to the olive oil.)

The pizza can be served immediately or returned to the oven, directly on the pizza stone, for 2 minutes to crisp a perfectly crunchy golden brown crust on the bottom. If the top requires more baking, use the broiler. Once the pizza is completely baked, slice and top with unbaked ingredients like cured meats, salad greens, fresh seasonal vegetables, finely grated hard cheeses, finishing oils, fresh herbs, artisan salt, or freshly ground pepper. Use a two-handled pizza cutter and fast, decisive movements to yield clean cuts.

To reheat leftovers: If you like leftover pizza, you'll really love this dough. Chill or freeze any leftover pizza, tightly wrapped. Allow the pizza to come back to room temperature, then reheat individual slices in a preheated, covered, nonstick or cast-iron pan for 5 to 10 minutes on low heat. Larger slabs of pizza can be reheated in the oven on the pizza stone for 5 to 10 minutes.

TOPPINGS

A Slow Rise Pizza most often resembles a reconstructed charcuterie board with bites of different textures and temperatures: roasted vegetables, grated hard cheeses, olives or pickled vegetables, cured meats, and soft cheeses all piled vertically and draped architecturally. The most delicate toppings, like prosciutto or burrata, are always added after the bake. Everything gets a pinch of artisan salt, fresh cracked pepper, and olive oil. Brohner rarely uses sauce. Or he opts for a sparse tableau, letting the crust shine under a luxuriant drizzle of very, very good extra-virgin olive oil and crunchy crystals of finishing salt.

This being *The L.A. Cookbook*, all the resources are here for you to capture the tastes of this magnificent city. Given the communal experience of L.A. shopping, cooking, dining, and eating, there had to be a way to tie these ideas together, and pizza is our answer. With this dough in the refrigerator, you can sustainably repurpose many of the recipes in this book, singly or in combinations. Borrowing bits and pieces from all these great restaurants, you can assemble an all-new cuisine, as delicious as it is diverse. I can't think of anything more L.A. than that.

1
Fennel Sausage
Tuscan Kale
Bread Crumbs
Fennel Pollen
(LOVE & SALT page 123)
Onion Soubise
(TROIS MEC page 204)

2
Tomato Coulis
(BADMAASH page 135)
Turkey Meatloaf crumbles
(AMMO page 167)
Ricotta
Oregano

3
Smoked Mozzarella
Shredded Latkes
(WEXLER'S page 75)
Fried Egg
Rosemary

4
Pineapple Kimchi
(BAROO page 179)
Speck
Warm Country Ham Vinaigrette
(HATCHET HALL page 68)
Mozarella
Jalapeño Slices

5
Stinging Nettle
Pecorino or Mozzarella
Shaved Red Onion
Pickled Fennel
(AUGUSTINE page 191)

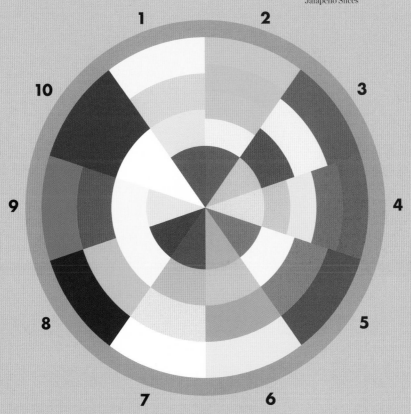

6
Halloumi
Charred Lemon
(LINCOLN page 102)
Pistachio Salsa Verde
(FARMSHOP page 37)
Chopped Avocado

7
Cultured Nut Cheese
(MOON JUICE page 55)
Lavender
Honey
Red Chili Oil

8
Blackened Radicchio
(ELF CAFÉ page 180)
Pancetta
Fontina
Fried Rosemary
(PORRIDGE + PUFFS page 71)

9
Broccolini Agliolio
(CROSSROADS page 109)
Calabrian Chile
Sheep's-Milk Ricotta
Bread Crumbs

10
Berry Pie Filling
(RUCKER'S PIE page 227)
Whipped Cream
(SPAGO page 218)

MARINE LAYER

FISH AND SEAFOOD

Badmaash
Salmon Boti Kabob with Spiced Tomato Coulis

Rosaliné
Striped Bass Ceviche, Aji Amarillo Leche de Tigre

Covell
Tuna Conserva

The Tasting Kitchen
Salt-Crusted Branzino alla Puttanesca

The Little Door
Roasted Bacon-Wrapped Monkfish with Roasted Romanesco, Blood Orange-Caper Sauce, and Cauliflower-Mustard Mash

Bombo
Curried Shrimp Bowl

L & E Oyster Bar
Oysters Rockefeller

Matsuhisa
Black Cod in Miso

The Hungry Cat
Chorizo & Clams with Braised Tuscan Kale and Soffritto

Badmaash / Salmon Boti Kabob with Spiced Tomato Coulis

Badmaash has a split personality between straight-up regional Indian and a modern city gastropub. That, friends, is how DTLA got its very own chicken *tikka* poutine, a wild explosion of zeitgeisty, gustatory pleasures, and this crowd-pleaser. The word *boti* describes large chunks of meat in the Indian *dhaba* (casual eateries, such as roadside restaurants). Typically it's lamb or goat, but expect the unexpected in Los Angeles: a thick cut of salmon, cubed, and crazy charred. At Badmaash, they cook the salmon in the tandoori oven, where the salmon is "kissed" by an open flame. The broiler modification approaches that charred idea for a home kitchen. You can easily use an open grill, charbroiler, or even finish this with a kitchen torch to go the distance. It's light and bright, delicious with a side of rice or bread to sop up the sweet, spiced tomato coulis.

SERVES 4 TO 6

TOMATO COULIS
2 tablespoons olive oil

1 teaspoon nigella seeds (*kalonji*)

6 to 8 whole peeled plum tomatoes, pureed

½ teaspoon red chile powder

2 tablespoons sugar

1 tablespoon red wine vinegar

½ teaspoon salt

SALMON BOTI
1 cup plain yogurt

1 tablespoon finely chopped fresh ginger

1 tablespoon finely chopped garlic

½ cup chopped dill

Zest and juice of 1 medium lime

1 teaspoon red wine vinegar

1 teaspoon Dijon mustard

1 teaspoon red chile powder

1 tablespoon chickpea flour

1 teaspoon (3 grams) Diamond Crystal kosher salt

1 tablespoon olive oil

2 pounds skin-on salmon fillet, scaled and deboned

Fresh lime wedges, for garnish

Cilantro leaves, for garnish

To make the tomato coulis: In a medium skillet, heat the olive oil over medium heat. Add the nigella seeds and lightly toast until their aromatics are released. Add the tomato puree and red chile powder, and stir to combine. Add the sugar and vinegar, and cook until hot, stirring gently to blend the flavors. Remove from the heat, season with the salt, and set aside.

To prepare the salmon *boti*: In a bowl, whisk the yogurt until smooth. Whisk in the ginger, garlic, dill, lime zest and juice, vinegar, mustard, red chile powder, chickpea flour, salt, and olive oil.

Cut the salmon into 2-inch cubes (about the size of baby alphabet blocks). Toss them with the yogurt mixture. Cover and marinate in the refrigerator for 5 to 6 hours.

Preheat the broiler or preheat the oven to 500°F. Oil a baking pan.

Place the salmon in the pan, skin-side down. Broil for 5 minutes. Be mindful; it can burn quickly at such a high temperature. Remove from the oven and, if not charred on top, use a kitchen torch to finish.

To assemble: Plate the salmon with the warm tomato coulis, lime wedges, and whole leaves of cilantro. Serve immediately.

Rosaliné / Striped Bass Ceviche, Aji Amarillo Leche de Tigre

Ceviche (*cebiche*, if we're in Peru) is a genius party appetizer. It's fresh; it's zesty. Friends who "should" themselves mercilessly about eating healthy gobble it down. Amped up with the fruity Peruvian *aji amarillo* pepper, *leche de tigre* ("tiger's milk") is the intense citrus base, courtesy of chef Ricardo Zarate.

Two keys to success are to use the *leche de tigre* as soon as you make it and to purchase sashimi-grade seafood from the fishmonger. Chef Zarate calls for striped bass, but any lean white fish—think sea bass, halibut, mahi mahi—works. When you're squeezing the limes, the juice gets bitter as you squeeze deeper, so best to buy a few more limes than you'd think you need and treat them lightly. Traditionally, the ceviche is paired with *crocante* fried calamari—add your own make-ahead crunch by serving with potato chips, corn chips, or on tostadas.

SERVES 4

1 pound striped bass

LECHE DE TIGRE
1 large garlic clove, minced
1 small piece fresh ginger (about ½ inch), peeled and coarsely chopped
½ celery stalk, thinly sliced
2 tablespoons finely chopped red onion
1½ tablespoons *aji amarillo* paste
¾ cup fresh lime juice
1½ tablespoons (13 grams) Diamond Crystal kosher salt
5 small ice cubes

TO ASSEMBLE
½ medium red onion, thinly sliced
Salt
Fresh lime juice, to taste
½ cup roughly chopped fresh cilantro

Cut the bass into small cubes. Reserve 2 tablespoons for the *leche de tigre*; cover and refrigerate the remainder until ready to serve.

To make the *leche de tigre*: In a blender, combine the reserved 2 tablespoons chopped fish with the garlic, ginger, celery, onion, *aji amarillo* paste, and a few tablespoons of the lime juice. Puree until well combined. With the blender running, add the salt, then very slowly pour in the remaining lime juice until the sauce emulsifies. With the blender still running, add the ice cubes, one at a time, until the sauce is smooth and frothy. Cover and refrigerate for up to 1 hour.

To assemble: In a medium bowl, combine the cubed fish and 1 cup of the chilled *leche de tigre*. Using clean hands (to keep the fish from breaking), gently toss until well coated, then add the red onion and toss again. Taste and adjust the seasoning with salt and lime juice—you want it puckery. Into the center of a shallow bowl, spoon the ceviche and sprinkle the cilantro on top.

Covell / Tuna Conserva

L.A. *loves* its toasts, and this poached fish recipe is tartine-ready. At Covell, it's served as a bar snack with tomato-smeared crostini, but that's only the beginning. Stuff a giant tuna melt with pickled fennel (page 191); mix it into a dip, or boil eggs, potatoes, and green beans, Castelvetrano olives, and with a lemony vinaigrette (page 102), you're well on your way to a killer niçoise salad.

If fresh albacore is not available, substitute good-quality, imported oil-packed tuna and skip the oven-poaching step. When poaching, monitor the oven and drop the temperature a little if you see too much activity in the oil—the idea is not to boil the tuna.

MAKES 1 POUND

1 pound fresh albacore tuna, bloodline and skin removed, cut into 2 pieces

2 cups olive oil

Juice of 1 lemon

½ medium red onion, cut into small dice

¼ cup Dijon mustard

2 tablespoons chopped parsley

12 pitted olives, rinsed and chopped

2 tablespoons chopped pepperoncini

Salt and freshly ground black pepper

Preheat the oven to 325°F.

Put the albacore tuna and olive oil in a small pan so the fish is completely submerged. Poach in the oven for 30 minutes. You want to see some bubbles rising up in the oil, but it should not be simmering.

When the tuna is ready, remove it from the oven and let cool completely in the oil.

Break up the tuna into very large flakes, reserving the oil. In a medium bowl, mix the flaked tuna with the lemon juice, onion, mustard, parsley, olives, and pepperoncini. Pour in ¼ cup of the poaching oil and mix until completely combined, adding more, if needed. You want it slightly on the oily side. Season lightly and serve it room temperature or chilled, or refrigerate it in an airtight container for up to a week.

The Tasting Kitchen / Salt-Crusted Branzino alla Puttanesca

With the arrival of Casey Lane and The Tasting Kitchen, you knew magic arrived on Abbot Kinney in the form of housemade tinctures; wildly funky wines introduced to curious palates; and nightly menus punched out on typewriter and stenciled with numbers.

The key here is simplicity. This theatrical entrée requires cracking open a hard salt shell to reveal the tender, flaky perfectly cooked fish underneath. The bright, sunny notes of tomato, olive, and fragrant olive oil feel seasonal, though it's a pantry dish at heart. Coarse rock salt or kosher salt won't make the fish overly sticky or salty—but fine sea salt will. And yes, you can tell your guests that *alla puttanesca* does, in fact, translate to "whore's sea bass."

SERVES 2

SALT-CRUSTED BRANZINO
24 ounces coarse rock salt (or coarse kosher salt), plus more as needed
1 egg white
2½ tablespoons sugar
1 (1-pound) whole branzino, cleaned
3 or 4 tarragon sprigs
3 or 4 thyme sprigs

PUTTANESCA
2 tablespoons olive oil
½ teaspoon finely minced garlic
½ teaspoon finely minced anchovy
Small pinch of chopped rosemary
3 or 4 chiles de árbol, thinly julienned
½ cup (4 ounces) chicken stock
1 tablespoon butter
1 teaspoon capers
1 teaspoon niçoise olives, soaked in fresh water and halved
2 tablespoons julienned oven-dried or sun-dried tomatoes
Finely chopped parsley, for garnish
1 lemon, cut into eighths and seeded
Fruity extra-virgin olive oil (preferably Arbequina), for garnish

To prepare the salt-crusted branzino: Preheat the oven to 400°F.

In a large bowl, combine the salt, egg white, and sugar and mix until it reaches the consistency of damp sand. Do not overmix (this will whip the egg white from the friction with the salt). Cover the bottom of a baking pan with a thick, even layer of the salt mixture.

Stuff the cleaned fish with the tarragon and thyme. Rest the branzino on the salt, making sure it doesn't touch the sides or bottom of the pan. Cover the fish entirely with the rest of the salt mixture, leaving just the head and tail exposed. Pat down to form a crust.

Bake for 25 minutes, or until the salt begins to brown. Remove from the oven and allow the fish to rest for 6 to 10 minutes.

After the fish has rested, crack the salt crust with a mallet or the handle of a heavy knife. Using a wide spatula, gently transfer the fish to a platter. Remove and discard the thyme and tarragon. Using a paring knife (or your fingers), starting at the tail and working toward the head, carefully peel off the skin. Be careful not to remove the collarbone. When you finish one side, flip it very gently using the spatula and your hand so the fish does not fall apart, and repeat with the second side.

To make the puttanesca: In a small pan, warm 1 tablespoon of the olive oil over medium heat until hot but not smoking. Add the garlic, anchovy, rosemary, and chiles. Sweat, stirring often, until cooked and fragrant but not browned, about 30 seconds. Pour in the stock and cook until the liquid has reduced by two-thirds. Once the liquid has reduced, add the butter to the pan, and swirl until the butter has fully melted and is incorporated into the sauce. Add the capers, olives, dried tomatoes, and parsley and stir until just incorporated. Season the sauce with juice from 2 of the lemon segments. Drizzle with the remaining 1 tablespoon olive oil.

To assemble: While still hot, spoon the puttanesca sauce over the cleaned branzino. Serve the fish on the platter, with the remaining lemon segments and some fruity olive oil.

The Little Door / Roasted Bacon-Wrapped Monkfish with Roasted Romanesco, Blood Orange-Caper Sauce, and Cauliflower-Mustard Mash

As popular now as it was when it opened two decades ago, this twinkling Mediterranean-inspired wonderland hides behind its titular wooden doors. Those hinges have been well worked by Angelenos toasting many a birthday or three-picture deal with harissa-spiked mezze platters and spanakopita. Either could kick off a meal starring this bacon-wrapped monkfish and trippy looking romanesco. When blood oranges aren't available, imported blood orange juice is a painless substitution.

SERVES 2

Salt

1 head romanesco, trimmed into florets

8 tablespoons extra-virgin olive oil

1 onion, finely diced

1 head cauliflower, trimmed and thinly sliced

Freshly ground black pepper

Freshly grated nutmeg

3 tablespoons whole-grain mustard

2 tablespoons chopped flat-leaf parsley

1 medium shallot, finely chopped

½ cup dry white wine

1 cup blood orange juice (from about 4 blood oranges)

4 tablespoons cold butter (½ stick), cut into pieces

Juice of ½ lemon

2 tablespoons capers, coarsely chopped

4 (2½-ounce) monkfish medallions

4 slices bacon or pancetta

Bring a medium pot of salted water to a boil. Fill a large bowl with ice and water and set aside. Blanch the romanesco until al dente, about 2 minutes. Immediately dunk them into the ice bath to cool, then drain. Set aside.

In a medium pot, warm 3 tablespoons of the olive oil over medium-low heat. Add the onion, cover, and cook until translucent, stirring occasionally, 6 to 8 minutes. Reduce the heat to low. Add the cauliflower and stir well. Season with salt, pepper, and a dash of nutmeg. Once the onion and cauliflower have softened, gently fold in the mustard, parsley, and 2 tablespoons of the remaining olive oil. The cauliflower will begin to fall apart as you mix.

In a separate small saucepan, combine the shallot, wine, and blood orange juice. Bring this mixture to a simmer over medium-low heat, then cook until the liquid has almost completely evaporated. Reduce the heat to low. Slowly whisk in the butter, bit by bit, to create an emulsion. Once the butter is fully incorporated and the sauce looks richer, add the lemon juice and capers and stir well. Check the seasoning. Keep warm.

Preheat the oven to 375°F. Trim the monkfish medallions of any gray membranes. Season both sides with salt and pepper, and wrap each medallion with a slice of bacon. Skewer with a toothpick to hold in place, but don't wrap too tightly, as the bacon will shrink during cooking. Set aside on a plate.

In a large, oven-safe sauté pan, heat the remaining 3 tablespoons olive oil over medium-high heat until hot but not smoking. Quickly sear the bacon-wrapped monkfish and blanched romanesco for about 3 minutes. Brown the first side, then flip to match the coloring on the second side. Transfer the pan to the oven to roast for a final 5 minutes, or until the fish is cooked through and opaque.

To assemble: Spoon the warm cauliflower mash in the center of two plates. Pull the monkfish from the oven and set 2 medallions on each plate. Discard the toothpicks. Drizzle the reduction around the plate, and top with the romanesco. Serve immediately.

Bombo / Curried Shrimp Bowl

Chef Mark Peel is behind the steamy soups and stews of Grand Central Market's Bombo, his follow-up to the inimitable Campanile. Ladled over rice, this comforting shrimp bowl satisfies with a golden, creamy curry studded with cubes of potato, squash, and peanuts. It has "weekday dinner" written all over it. You can make the rice and chop the vegetables on a Sunday, marinate the shrimp in the easy-make curry before you leave for work, and just when you're home, tired, and feeling far too lazy to cook, remember that you can finish this dish in half the time it'd take for delivery.

SERVES 4

1 pound shrimp (21-25 count), deveined

6½ tablespoons curry powder

6 tablespoons olive oil

4 ounces yellow onion (about 1 small onion), thinly sliced

¾ pound red rose (or red) potatoes, cut into small dice

¼ pound kabocha squash, cut into small dice

¾ cup chicken broth

¾ cup heavy cream

2 tablespoons sriracha

½ cup chopped unsalted peanuts, toasted or roasted

2 tablespoons chopped parsley, for garnish

Steamed white or brown rice, for serving

Salt and freshly ground black pepper

In a bowl or zip-top bag, toss the shrimp with 4½ tablespoons of the curry powder. Cover and refrigerate for at least 1 hour.

To prepare the curry: In a large cast-iron pan, warm the olive oil over medium heat until hot but not smoking. Add the onion, potatoes, and squash and cook, stirring, until the potatoes and squash are fork-tender, 6 to 8 minutes. Once the vegetables are ready, pour in the broth and cream and stir. Add the sriracha and the remaining 2 tablespoons curry powder, and stir to combine. Simmer for 3 minutes, then add the shrimp and peanuts. Cover the skillet and simmer for 3 minutes, or until the shrimp are opaque and fully cooked through.

To assemble: Spoon ½ cup of steamed rice into each of four bowls. Ladle the shrimp curry stew on top. Garnish with chopped parsley and season with salt and pepper.

L & E Oyster Bar / Oysters Rockefeller

One would expect a nacreous bivalve named after a Rockefeller to be rich, right? Indeed, the broiled and baked New Orleans hallmark of Antoine's restaurant is nothing if not heart stopping. The pro shuckers at Silverlake's L & E Oyster Bar give the ultra-rich New Orleans classic a shot of West Coast style by tucking oysters under a spinach-garlic blanket and grilling them to a delicious finish equal parts smoky, herby, and briny.

Freeze logs of the composed butter ahead of time and slice dabs onto just-shucked oysters before tossing on the grill for an impromptu beachside feast. It also makes a great topping to roast anything—from fingerling potatoes to salmon to snails. If you're a lemonhead, serve with Lincoln's charred lemon wedge (page 102).

MAKES 24

¼ cup olive oil

5 garlic cloves, sliced

½ white onion, finely diced

Zest of 3 lemons

1 cup white wine

½ cup fresh spinach, washed

1 cup (2 sticks) unsalted butter, at room temperature

Juice of 3 lemons

2 cups grated Gruyère cheese

Salt and freshly ground black pepper

24 oysters, shucked but still attached to bottom shell

1 cup bread crumbs

Lemon wedges, for serving

In a sauté pan, heat the olive oil over high heat. Add the garlic and cook, stirring frequently, until golden brown. Add the onion and lemon zest and cook for 5 minutes. Carefully pour in the wine, then increase the heat to high and bring to a boil, scraping up any browned bits with a wooden spoon. After the wine has reduced by half, turn off the heat and add the spinach, tossing with tongs till wilted. Spread the mixture evenly onto a baking sheet to cool.

On a clean work surface, set out a large piece of plastic wrap. In a food processor, blitz the cooled spinach mixture with the butter and lemon juice until smooth, about 1 minute. Stop the machine, scrape down the sides, and add the Gruyère. Process for 1 minute more, then season with salt and pepper. Scrape the mixture into the plastic wrap. Wrap tightly, rolling into a compact log. Freeze until ready for use. (Alternatively, refrigerate the mixture in an airtight container until set.)

To assemble: Heat a grill to high. Spoon tablespoon-size dabs of the spinach-butter mixture into each oyster. Place the shells directly on the grates and grill until the outside of the oysters curls up and the butter has melted. Remove with tongs and top each with a sprinkle of bread crumbs. Serve while hot.

Matsuhisa / Black Cod in Miso

You might not guess that the unassuming front on La Cienega's restaurant row has long concealed the launch pad for a global empire of sushi and Japanese cuisine. Nobu Matsuhisa's flagship, Matsuhisa, has given us oft-imitated signatures whose names and flavors we know by heart. Among them, Nobu's famous miso black cod—charred, silky, flaky, sweet, complex, delicate, and rich, all at once. It's a two-day marinade, but you can accelerate the process overnight with excellent results.

The combination of sake, mirin, white miso, and sugar is a saucy secret weapon. This recipe yields 3 cups and will keep in the fridge for a while, so try using the sweet miso paste in dessert applications, too. Turn to the pickled ginger we know and love because the only stumper here might be *hajikami*, the long pickled ginger shoots with hot fuchsia bottoms—elusive even in L.A.'s well-stocked Japanese supermarkets.

SERVES 4

¾ cup sake

¾ cup mirin

2 cups white miso paste

1 cup sugar

4 (8-ounce) black cod fillets

4 stalks *hajikami* (sweet vinegar-pickled ginger), cleaned and cut into 6-inch lengths

In a medium saucepan, bring the sake and mirin to a boil over high heat. Cook for 20 seconds to evaporate the alcohol, then reduce the heat to low. Mix in the miso paste. Once the miso has dissolved completely, raise the heat to high. Add the sugar, stirring continuously with a wooden spoon to prevent scorching. The sauce should begin to thin. As soon as the sugar has dissolved completely, remove from the heat and let cool to room temperature. The sauce can be refrigerated and kept for up to a week.

Pat the cod dry with paper towels. Slather the fish with the cooled marinade and place in a nonreactive dish or bowl. You'll need a few drops for garnish, but reserve the remaining *saikyo miso* in an airtight container for other uses. Cover tightly with plastic wrap and refrigerate overnight or up to 2 days.

Preheat the broiler. Line the broiler pan with aluminum foil.

Lightly wipe any excess marinade clinging to the fillets, but don't rinse. Discard the remaining marinade. Place the cod on the prepared pan skin-side down and broil for 2 minutes, or until the surface of the fish begins to brown so deep as to almost blacken. Promptly turn off the broiler and set the oven to 400°F. Bake for 10 to 12 minutes, until opaque and flaky. (Begin checking the fish after 8 minutes.) Transfer to plates and garnish with the *hajikami*. Add a few drops of the refrigerated miso to the plate and serve while hot.

The Hungry Cat / Chorizo & Clams with Braised Tuscan Kale and Soffritto

An ideal Sunday supper is to throw down old pages of the *L.A. Times* across the table and dole out oversized bowls of this soul-satisfying L.A.-style surf 'n' turf. David Lentz's Chorizo & Clams is what I consider a bona fide "restaurant" recipe: It's prepped ahead of time and assembles in the precious minutes it takes for the clams to open. The base techniques for the soffritto, chickpeas, and braised kale are clutch concepts for your repertoire. Release the aromatics from a chile de árbol and rosemary sprig, sweat onions and garlic, deglaze with sherry—you'll need 2 quarts for this recipe, but it's worth it—and braise. For the sake of convenience, I've substituted cooked (canned) chickpeas here. Bonus: The cast-iron grilling method for Go Get Em Tiger's panzanella croutons (page 186) makes an ideal toast to soak up all the delicious broth with Lincoln's romesco (page 102).

SERVES 4

OLIVE OIL-BRAISED SOFFRITTO
1 cup extra-virgin olive oil plus 1½ tablespoons
1 chile de árbol
½ sprig rosemary
2 cups diced white onions
1 cup sliced garlic
2 cups chopped red bell peppers
4 cups sherry
1½ teaspoons hot paprika
Salt

BRAISED TUSCAN KALE
1 bunch Tuscan kale, ribs removed
3 tablespoons extra-virgin olive oil, plus more if needed
1 chile de árbol
1 sprig rosemary
½ white onion, sliced
2½ garlic cloves, minced
Salt and freshly ground black pepper

To make the soffritto: In a heavy pot, warm 1½ tablespoons of the olive oil over medium heat. Once hot but not smoking, add the chile and rosemary. Cook, stirring, for 1 minute, or until fragrant. Add the onions, garlic, and bell peppers, then reduce the heat to medium-low, and sweat them gently until translucent, about 5 minutes. If you hear sizzling, reduce the heat. Once the onions are translucent, carefully pour in the sherry. Raise the heat to high and scrape up any browned bits from the bottom of the pan with a wooden spoon. Cook until the liquid has almost completely reduced and the pan looks dry. Add the hot paprika, season with salt, and add the remaining 1 cup olive oil. Cook the soffritto over low heat, stirring occasionally, for 1 hour, until the vegetables are very soft. Set aside.

To braise the kale: Bring a pot of salted water to a boil. Fill a large bowl with ice and water and set it in the sink. Blanch the kale for 30 seconds, then immediately drain and plunge it into the ice water. Remove and squeeze all the water out.

In a heavy pot, warm 2 tablespoons of the olive oil over medium heat. Once warmed but not smoking, add the chile and rosemary. Cook, stirring, for 1 minute, or until fragrant. Add the onion and garlic, then reduce the heat to medium-low and sweat gently until translucent, about 5 minutes. Mix in the blanched kale with tongs, and season with salt and black pepper. Add the remaining 1 tablespoon olive oil, cover, and braise over very low heat for up to 1 hour, checking every 10 minutes, until the oil has been absorbed and the kale is very soft. If it becomes too dry, add more oil. Set aside.

CONTINUED

Chorizo & Clams with Braised Tuscan Kale and Soffritto

CONTINUED

TO ASSEMBLE

2½ tablespoons extra-virgin olive oil

1½ cups Mexican (uncured) chorizo

1½ cups drained cooked (or canned) chickpeas

60 manila clams, picked over and cleaned

4 cups sherry

2 cups chicken stock

2 tablespoons butter

Juice of ½ medium lemon

1 tablespoon chopped parsley

4 thick slices of bread, grilled

2 tablespoons aioli or mayonnaise

Salt and freshly ground black pepper

To assemble: In a large, heavy pot, warm the olive oil over medium heat. Add the chorizo and cook, breaking up large pieces. When the color of the meat begins to turn opaque, add 1 cup of the soffritto and allow it to warm. Add the chickpeas and stir until combined. Stir in 1 cup of the braised kale. Add the clams. Pour in the sherry, then raise the heat to high and bring to a boil. Scrape up any browned bits with a wooden spoon. Reduce the heat slightly, cover, and simmer for 5 to 7 minutes (about the time it takes for the clams to open). Pour in the stock and bring to a simmer. Add the butter, season with salt, and reduce the heat to low. Add the lemon juice and check the seasoning. As soon as the butter has melted, take the pot off the heat.

Set bowls for empty clamshells on the table. Ladle the stew into bowls and top with a sprinkle of parsley and a generous dab of aioli or mayonnaise, and the grilled toast.

THE BIG ONE

MAIN DISHES

Cliff's Edge
Sunday Adobo Chicken with Mole Sauce

La Casita Mexicana
Mole de Pistache

Animal
Balsamic Barbecued Baby-Back Ribs

Revolutionario
Black-Eyed Pea Falafel Tacos

Son of a Gun
Fried Chicken Sandwich, Spicy B&B Pickle Slaw, Rooster Aioli

Guelaguetza
Mole Amarillo de Pollo

Ammo
Turkey Meatloaf with Ammo Ketchup

Redbird
Grilled Lamb Loin with Kimchi Pancake and Sumac Yogurt

Park's BBQ
Beef Bulgogi

Everson Royce Bar
The Bar Burger

Cliff's Edge / Sunday Adobo Chicken with Mole Sauce

There's no way to publish a California cookbook without a lovely roasted chicken recipe. Whether herbed, lemony, garlic-rubbed, or spiced, it captures the throwback West Coast vibes of Sunday supper. Brined in the method chef Mike Bryant outlines, you avoid the pitfalls of a gummy, pulpy, or rubbery bird. Rustic slabs of seasoned heirloom tomatoes or sautéed mushrooms provide simple market garnishes. With a bottle of pinot on the table, it'll match the twinkling spell cast on the tree-canopied patio at Cliff's Edge in Silverlake, where all you want to do is linger.

Given his playful, technique-driven repertoire of world flavors, it makes sense that Bryant's recipe references both adobo and an ambrosial take on Oaxacan mole. Vinegary adobo (*adobar* means "to marinate") was once a preservation method; today, it's more of a spiced paste. Instead of cooking the meat with the soy and vinegar and spices, Bryant blitzes his variation into a wet rub. The mole, preferably made ahead while the chicken brines, is served as a sauce. Bryant included an extra portion of adobo in the recipe to refrigerate for your next barbecue. (If you've never slow-cooked a pork shoulder in a *caja china*, here's your shot.)

SERVES 4

CHICKEN AND BRINE

1 gallon cold water

1 cup (140 grams) Diamond Crystal kosher salt

1 whole head garlic, sliced crosswise

1 tablespoon whole black peppercorns, toasted

2 lemons, halved

5 bay leaves

10 thyme sprigs

1 whole roasting chicken, about 3½ pounds

Salt and freshly ground black pepper

MOLE

1 ancho chile

2 Thai chiles, stemmed

2 tablespoons vegetable oil

1 cup (4 ounces) peeled and coarsely chopped fresh ginger

6 ounces garlic, coarsely chopped (about 15 cloves, or 1 to 2 whole heads)

1 medium white onion, coarsely chopped

2 Roma (plum) tomatoes, chopped

¼ cup raisins

To brine the chicken: The night or morning before you plan on roasting your chicken, in a large roaster or stockpot, combine the cold water and salt and stir to dissolve. Add the garlic, peppercorns, lemon halves and juice, bay leaves, and thyme. Gently submerge the chicken and chill for about 8 hours or up to overnight. (More time is not necessarily better; over-brining will lead to a gummy texture.)

To make the mole: Preheat the oven to 400°F.

Place the chiles on a baking sheet and roast until blackened and crispy, about 5 minutes on each side. Transfer the chiles to a clean cutting surface. Remove the seeds and coarsely chop or break them apart with your hands. Set aside.

In a large stockpot, warm the vegetable oil over medium-high heat until hot but not smoking. Add the ginger, garlic, onion, and tomatoes. Reduce the heat slightly and sweat, stirring, until the onions are translucent, about 8 minutes. Add the chiles to the mixture and stir. Add the raisins, almonds, pumpkin seeds, cumin, cloves, and sesame seeds, then reduce the heat to low. Cook for 10 minutes, stirring frequently to avoid scorching the bottom of the pan.

Carefully pour in the wine and cook over medium-low heat until the liquid reduces by about two-thirds, 10 to 15 minutes. Pour in the stock, soy sauce, truffle oil (if using), and vinegar. A bit

CONTINUED

Sunday Adobo Chicken with Mole Sauce

CONTINUED

½ cup almonds, roasted or toasted

½ cup hulled pumpkin seeds, roasted or toasted

1 teaspoon cumin seeds

5 whole cloves

¼ cup black sesame seeds

½ (750-ml) bottle red wine (preferably Burgundy or light, dry pinot noir)

4 cups chicken stock

½ cup soy sauce

1 tablespoon truffle oil (optional)

1 tablespoon sherry vinegar

3 ounces dark chocolate (64% cacao), coarsely chopped

Zest of 1 lemon

5 parsley sprigs

5 cilantro sprigs

Leaves of 5 thyme sprigs, plus more for garnish

Salt and freshly ground black pepper

ADOBO RUB

⅔ cup soy sauce

2 tablespoons distilled white vinegar

1 tablespoon garlic powder

1 tablespoon onion powder

1 teaspoon ground turmeric

2 bay leaves

2 teaspoons brown sugar

2 teaspoons paprika

3 large mint leaves

4 cilantro sprigs

1⅓ cups blended oil (75-25% canola/olive oil blend)

Thyme leaves, for garnish

Heirloom tomatoes (optional)

at a time, add in the chocolate, stirring as it melts, until fully incorporated. Add the lemon zest, parsley, cilantro, and thyme. Simmer, allowing the mole to reduce by half, about 20 minutes.

Transfer the mole to a blender and, being careful with the hot mixture, puree until smoothie-thick. Season with salt and black pepper. Allow the mole to cool to room temperature before refrigerating. (The mole will be best the next day.)

To make the adobo rub: In a clean blender or food processor, combine all the rub ingredients except the blended oil. Blitz until smooth. Stop the motor and scrape down the sides. While the motor is running, slowly drizzle in the blended oil until you reach a very thick, pasty consistency, and set aside.

To roast the chicken: Preheat the oven to 400°F.

Remove the chicken from the brine, and dump the brine. Pat the chicken dry but do not rinse. Rub the chicken liberally with the adobo, inside and out, and season well with salt and pepper.

Set a rack on top of a rimmed baking sheet or roasting pan. Set the chicken on the rack, breast-side up. Roast until you reach an internal temperature of 165°F near the thigh bone, anywhere from 45 minutes to 1½ hours. Begin checking the temperature at 45 minutes, but not too often, or you'll let out all the heat. If the skin begins to darken too quickly or burn, tent the chicken with foil as you finish roasting.

To assemble: While the chicken roasts, reheat the mole in a small saucepan over low heat. Remove the finished chicken from the oven and allow the bird to rest for at least 10 minutes before carving. Spoon the mole over the bottom of a large serving platter and top with the chicken. Garnish with thyme leaves and, if in season, heirloom tomatoes. Serve while hot.

La Casita Mexicana / Mole de Pistache

Tart and acidic from the tomatillo, and rich from pistachio, the striking green of this mole contrasts the bright orange on the walls at the cheerful La Casita Mexicana in the suburb of Bell. Use it as a thick blanket for proteins like pork medallions, roasted turkey and cheese crêpes.

Roasting tomatillos mellows their pucker out a little, giving this mole a rounder flavor than salsa verde. When selecting tomatillos at the market, look for a tight paper husk. The grayer they are, the longer they've been sitting out.

MAKES ABOUT 4 CUPS

3 pounds tomatillos, husked
2 serrano chiles, stemmed
1 red onion, thinly sliced
4 garlic cloves
¼ cup extra-virgin olive oil
1 tablespoon ground cinnamon
2 whole cloves
2 teaspoons cumin seeds, toasted
3 cups chicken stock
1½ cups roasted shelled pistachios
1 cup cilantro leaves
Salt

Preheat the oven to 375°F. Line a baking sheet with foil.

Wash the tomatillos to remove their sticky residue, pat dry, and slice into wedges. Combine in a large bowl with the chiles, red onion, and garlic, and toss with the olive oil till well coated. Spread the vegetables on the prepared baking sheet and roast until deeply charred but not burnt, about 25 minutes. Keep an eye on them and shake the pan every few minutes.

Transfer the charred vegetables to a large saucepan. Add the spices and stock and bring the mixture to a simmer over medium heat. Cook, stirring occasionally, until the vegetables are tender, about 10 minutes. Add the pistachios and simmer 10 more minutes.

Carefully transfer the hot mixture to a blender and puree. With the machine running, add the cilantro and continue to puree until smooth. Season with salt. Serve while hot.

Animal / Balsamic Barbecued Baby-Back Ribs

With their foie gras moco loco and these finger-or-fork ribs, the chefs known as Jon and Vinny, or "the Animal guys," brought a rustic warmth to L.A. for which diners readily ditched their dressing-on-the-side inclinations. Best that it all happened on a block of rock 'n' roll Fairfax, that cultural crossroads where Jewish delis mingle with skaters shopping for high-end streetwear.

Hardly shy, this signature dish steals the show at a potluck. Just because the word *barbecue* is in the name doesn't mean you need a giant smoker in the backyard. The oven preparation adapts wonderfully. All these ribs take is time—slow roasting and a damn fine beer barbecue sauce to slather on for a final broil. Comfort food sides such as Salazar's garlicky *esquites* (page 49), Jar's creamed spinach (page 183), or Maple Block's mac & cheese (page 110) are all natural matches. You might try a snappy salad like Terrine's shaved Brussels sprouts with dates and tart Pink Lady apples (page 193) for crunch.

SERVES 6 TO 8

2 racks pork baby-back ribs, halved

Canola or grapeseed oil, for rubbing

4 flat-leaf parsley sprigs

4 thyme sprigs

4 garlic cloves, smashed

Salt

BARBECUE SAUCE

1 cup ketchup (see page 167)

1 (12-ounce) bottle lager-style beer

½ cup balsamic vinegar

1 red onion, diced

1 garlic clove, very finely chopped

½ cup packed light brown sugar

3 tablespoons honey

1 ½ tablespoons grainy mustard

1 to 2 teaspoons hot sauce (to taste)

1 teaspoon Worcestershire sauce

¼ cup water

Preheat the oven to 500°F. Place each rib section on a 2-foot-long sheet of foil, shiny-side up. Rub each with oil and sprinkle with salt, then divide the herbs and garlic between the packets. Wrap the foil tightly around the ribs and place them in a roasting pan. Roast the ribs for 30 minutes, then reduce the oven temperature to 250°F. Cook until the ribs are fork-tender, about 90 minutes longer, to at least 180°F internal temperature.

Remove from the oven and carefully open the foil and rest the racks for 15 to 20 minutes, until cool enough to handle.

While the ribs roast, make the barbecue sauce: In a medium saucepan, whisk the ingredients together and bring to a boil over medium heat. Reduce the heat to medium-low and simmer for at least 1 hour, until it is thick and dense. (Animal sometimes slow-cooks the barbecue sauce for up to 3 hours, partially covered, for an intensely deep flavor.)

Set the oven to broil. Liberally brush the meaty side of the ribs with half the barbecue sauce. Broil the exposed ribs until caramelized and bubbling, 3 to 4 minutes. If you don't have a built-in broiler, then crank the oven temperature to 500°F and roast the ribs until the sauce is hot and bubbling.

To assemble: Transfer the ribs to a platter and serve with the remainder of barbecue sauce on the side.

Revolutionario / Black-Eyed Pea Falafel Tacos

Even in the taco-crawl town of Los Angeles, the North African tacos of Revolutionario offer elements of surprise. Served on homemade corn tortillas, sometimes griddled on a *comal* into a grilled cheese, chef Farid Zadi's falafels are a mash-up of West African *akara* fritters and Middle Eastern falafels blended with the tawny-hued Moroccan spice mix *ras el hanout*. While the small storefront is one of a kind, complete with a wall of signatures, you can still re-create some of the magic. Note that Revolutionario soaks their beans for two days to make extra-tender falafels, but overnight will also do fine.

MAKES ABOUT 20 FALAFEL

½ cup dried black-eyed peas
½ cup dried chickpeas
½ cup dried small red beans
6 garlic cloves
1 medium onion, coarsely chopped
2 green onions, white parts only
3 cilantro sprigs
3 parsley sprigs
Zest of 1 lemon
¼ cup fresh lemon juice, or to taste
½ teaspoon baking soda
½ teaspoon baking powder
1 tablespoon *ras el hanout* or Madras curry powder
½ teaspoon hot paprika
½ teaspoon freshly ground black pepper
1½ tablespoons salt, or to taste
5 cups vegetable oil, for frying

TO ASSEMBLE

Flatbreads or corn tortillas
Pico de gallo
Tahini sauce (page 56), optional
Sumac yogurt (page 168), optional
Pickled carrots and red onions, optional
Shaved radishes, optional
Pineapple-napa cabbage kimchi (page 179), optional

Put all the dried beans in a very large bowl or jar. Cover with water to fully submerge and allow for the beans to double in size. Refrigerate overnight or for up to 2 days.

Drain and rinse the beans. Transfer to a food processor. Working in batches, pulse until the beans have a rustic, nubby texture, scraping down the sides of the bowl as necessary. Don't over-process; the mixture shouldn't be smooth. Transfer the beans to a bowl and set aside.

Without washing out the processor bowl, combine all the remaining ingredients except the vegetable oil and process until smooth. Transfer to the bowl with the beans and stir until well combined.

Form the bean mixture into balls about the size of ping-pong balls (1½ inches or 2 tablespoons), by hand or with a falafel mold or cookie scoop.

Line a wire rack or plate with paper towels. In a cast-iron saucepan, heat the vegetable oil to 350°F. Test fry one falafel, frying for 4 to 5 minutes, and adjust the seasoning, if necessary, with salt and lemon juice. Using a slotted spoon or strainer, transfer to the rack.

When the oil returns to temperature, gently drop the falafel into the oil, one at a time. Without overcrowding, fry up to 5 at a time for 4 to 5 minutes, until the falafels are browned and cooked through in the center, not mealy. Transfer the falafels to the rack as they are finished to drain.

To assemble: Serve 2 per warmed flatbreads or corn tortilla, with any number of toppings such as pico de gallo, tahini sauce, sumac yogurt, pickled carrots and red onions, shaved radishes and pineapple-napa cabbage kimchi.

Son of a Gun / Fried Chicken Sandwich, Spicy B&B Pickle Slaw, Rooster Aioli

Only the few can join the elite ranks of Oakland's Bakesale Betty and Nashville's Acme Feed & Seed. But L.A. got its very own fried chicken sando winner when Jon Shook and Vinny Dotolo anchored their seafood-driven menu at Son of a Gun with straight-up turf. Diners have no shame in ordering seconds, so you may just want to go ahead and double this recipe. The hot sauce-mayo and sweet-spicy slaw are both dead easy to make. For a party, use smaller rolls, slice the breasts into tenders, and sling sliders.

File this life-hack away for the next time you're out of buttermilk: Stir 1 teaspoon white vinegar or lemon juice into whole milk and let stand for 5 minutes at room temperature.

MAKES 4

ROOSTER AIOLI
1 garlic clove, finely grated
½ cup mayonnaise
1 tablespoon Louisiana-style hot sauce

SPICY B&B PICKLE SLAW
½ small red onion, thinly sliced
1 jalapeño, thinly sliced
4 cups thinly sliced cabbage
½ cup bread-and-butter pickle slices
¼ cup pickle juice from the jar

FRIED CHICKEN
2 cups all-purpose flour
1 tablespoon freshly ground black pepper
½ teaspoon (1½ grams) Diamond Crystal kosher salt, plus more as needed
1 cup buttermilk
2 (8-ounce) boneless, skinless chicken breasts, halved crosswise
Peanut or vegetable oil, for frying

TO ASSEMBLE
4 white sandwich rolls, split
2 tablespoons butter, at room temperature

To make the aioli and slaw: Mix the garlic, mayonnaise, and hot sauce in a small bowl. Cover and chill. Toss the onion, jalapeño, cabbage, pickles, and pickle juice in a large bowl to combine. Cover and chill.

To fry the chicken: Set out two shallow bowls. Whisk the flour with the pepper and salt into the first. Into the second, pour the buttermilk. Working with 1 piece at a time, dredge the chicken in the flour mixture, shaking off any excess. Dip in the buttermilk, allowing any excess to drip back into the bowl. Dredge again, and again shake off any excess flour.

Pour oil into a large, heavy skillet to a depth of ½ inch and heat over medium heat to 350°F. Set a wire rack over a baking sheet lined with paper towels. Add the floured chicken to the hot oil and fry until golden brown and cooked through, about 3 minutes per side. Using a spatula, transfer pieces to the rack. Season to taste.

To assemble: Spread the cut sides of the rolls with butter. Heat a second skillet over medium heat. Working in batches, toast the rolls, buttered-side down, until browned and crisp, about 1 minute. Remove and spread with the spicy mayo. Build sandwiches on the rolls with chicken on the bottom, topped with the chilled slaw. Serve immediately.

Guelaguetza / Mole Amarillo de Pollo

The vast sprawl of Los Angeles feels like a bold galaxy of regional Mexican fare, including a rich constellation of Oaxacan moles. The inimitable Guelaguetza, run by the amazing Lopez family, might well be L.A.'s North Star. (Just look for the striking persimmon-hued mural by Colectivo Lapiztola outside.)

As far as the seven classic moles are concerned, lesser-known amarillo is especially family-friendly: Often prepared with chicken, it doesn't require laborious sourcing and is milder than its siblings. Masa, also the chief ingredient in tamales, thickens the stew. To grill the onions and garlic for this dish, wrap them in aluminum foil and place them directly over the heat until tender.

SERVES 4 TO 6

1 whole fryer chicken, 2½ to 3½ pounds

6 garlic cloves

1¼ medium onions

Salt

6 dried guajillo or Cascabel chiles

2 dried ancho chiles

1 chayote, quartered lengthwise

8 fingerling potatoes, or 4 medium potatoes, halved

½ teaspoon cumin seeds

10 whole black peppercorns

4 whole cloves

2 yerba santa leaves (or substitute ¼ teaspoon marjoram, ¼ teaspoon thyme, and 1 mint sprig)

1 cup warm water, plus more if needed

1 cup fresh masa

3 Roma (plum) tomatoes

3 tomatillos, husked

½ pound green beans

2 limes, cut into wedges, for serving

1 jalapeño, chopped, for garnish

2 garlic cloves, chopped, for garnish

Tortillas, for serving

Place the chicken, 3 of the garlic cloves, and ¼ onion in a large stockpot. Add 2 quarts water and lightly salt the water. Bring to a boil over medium-high heat. As soon as the water comes to a boil, reduce the heat to medium-low, cover, and let the chicken simmer until the meat is tender and opaque through the middle, the juices run clear when pierced, and an instant-read thermometer in the thickest part of the meat reads 165°F.

Meanwhile, in two separate bowls, soak the dried guajillo and ancho chiles in boiling water for 15 to 20 minutes, until softened.

Bring a separate stockpot full of water to a boil over medium heat. Add the chayote and potatoes, and boil until fork-tender, about 15 minutes. Drain and set aside.

Heat a dry cast-iron pan. Add the cumin seeds, peppercorns, and cloves. Toast the spices, shaking the pan until the aromatics are released, about 1 minute. Transfer to a molcajete or spice grinder and set aside. Return the pan to the heat, wiping it clean. Halve the 3 remaining garlic cloves and onion. Place them flat-side down in the pan and allow the surface to char undisturbed, about 5 minutes. Using tongs, remove and set aside.

Remove the poached chicken and discard the liquid, garlic, and onion. Cut the chicken into parts, or pull and chop the meat into pieces and reserve. Add the yerba santa leaves to the empty stockpot and set aside.

In a blender, add the warm water to the fresh masa. Blend until finely pureed. (Add another ½ cup water if it's sticking.) Strain this mixture into the stockpot with the leaves, place back on the heat, bring to a simmer, and simmer for 10 minutes, stirring continuously.

CONTINUED

Mole Amarillo de Pollo
CONTINUED

Without washing out the blender, puree the tomatoes, tomatillos, charred garlic, charred onion, and softened chiles. Pass through a fine strainer into the simmering masa mixture and stir attentively for 5 minutes.

Pound the toasted cumin, cloves, and peppercorns, and add the spice mix to the pot with additional salt. Simmer over medium-high heat for another 10 minutes, stirring occasionally.

Reduce the heat, and add the green beans, reserved cooked vegetables, and pulled chicken to the stockpot. Simmer for 5 minutes more. If the mole isn't thick enough to your liking, make another slurry of masa and warm water, and add, stirring continuously to prevent lumps from forming.

To assemble: Serve the mole in a bowl with a garnish of lime, chopped jalapeño, chopped garlic, and warm tortillas.

Ammo / Turkey Meatloaf with Ammo Ketchup

Ammo closed then reopened because of popular demand. (Thank you, Amy Sweeney!) Headlining the menu is and has always been the turkey meatloaf. Dense? Yes! No breadcrumbs here. A side of whipped potatoes and sautéed kale is the classic Ammo pairing. Leftovers make an admirable sandwich with ciabatta and a slab of melted Gruyère. I can promise Ammo's ketchup will enter your pantry repertoire and never leave.

SERVES 4 TO 6

AMMO KETCHUP

4 whole cloves, smashed

1 bay leaf

1 cinnamon stick

¼ teaspoon celery seeds

¼ teaspoon red pepper flakes

¼ teaspoon allspice berries

2 pounds tomatoes, coarsely chopped

1½ teaspoons (4½ grams) Diamond Crystal kosher salt, or to taste

½ cup distilled white vinegar, or to taste

¼ cup plus 1 tablespoon lightly packed brown sugar, or to taste

1 medium onion, chopped

1 Anaheim chile, chopped

1 garlic clove, smashed

TURKEY MEATLOAF

⅓ red bell pepper, coarsely chopped

⅓ yellow bell pepper, coarsely chopped

⅔ carrot, coarsely chopped

⅓ yellow onion, coarsely chopped

1 tablespoon olive oil

3 pounds ground dark meat turkey

3 eggs

Salt and freshly ground black pepper

To make the ketchup: Wrap the cloves, bay leaf, cinnamon stick, celery seeds, red pepper flakes, and allspice in a layer of cheesecloth, then tie into a bundle.

In a 4-quart saucepan, combine the spice sachet, tomatoes, salt, vinegar, brown sugar, onion, chile, and garlic. Cook over medium-high heat, stirring to combine, until the tomatoes have broken down and the onions and chiles are very soft, about 40 minutes. Remove and discard the spice bundle.

Transfer the mixture to a blender (don't wipe out the saucepan), then puree the sauce until smooth. Strain through a mesh strainer back into the same saucepan and return to medium heat. Cook, stirring occasionally, until thickened, about 30 minutes. Taste and add more salt, sugar, or vinegar, if desired. Transfer the ketchup to a glass jar and set aside to cool. (This will keep, covered, in the refrigerator for up to 3 weeks.)

To make the meatloaf: Preheat the oven to 350°F.

In a food processor, chop the bell peppers, carrot, and onion until fine. Warm the olive oil in a sauté pan over medium heat until hot but not smoking. Sweat the processed vegetables until just soft, 6 to 8 minutes. Remove from the heat and allow the vegetables to cool.

In a bowl, mix the ground turkey, cooled vegetables, and eggs until combined. Season generously with salt and black pepper, and add ½ cup of the ketchup. Mix until thoroughly incorporated, adding more ketchup if the mixture appears too crumbly and dry.

Grease a 10 by 12-inch metal baking pan or 9 by 5-inch two-piece "aerated" meatloaf pan. Pack the mixture into the pan, using a spatula to smooth the surface. Smack the pan hard on your counter to get rid of air bubbles. Brush with an additional thin layer of ketchup.

Bake for 40 minutes. Wiggle the pan a little, and if the meatloaf still looks a little loose, cook another 10 to 15 minutes before checking again. Bake until the meatloaf does not wiggle, the sauce has caramelized, and a thermometer inserted into the meatloaf registers 170°F, 50 to 55 minutes total.

To assemble: Transfer from oven to table. Serve slices of the meatloaf hot, with Ammo ketchup on the side.

Redbird / Grilled Lamb Loin with Kimchi Pancake and Sumac Yogurt

In downtown L.A.'s historic Vibiana church, L.A. native Neal Fraser continues to push the envelope with global flavors and sophistication. For this dish, kimchi and green onion have a meet-cute with a sweet potato pancake. Meanwhile, the tannic, lemony note of sumac in a cool whip of yogurt pivots this dish toward the East. (Sumac is the powdered garnet-hued fruit of its same-named bush—a terrific source of fruit acid, similar to tamarind.)

SERVES 4

LAMB LOIN
2 green onions, chopped
1 Fresno chile, coarsely chopped
2 garlic cloves
½ cup fresh orange juice
5 mint leaves
¼ cup olive oil
1 deboned lamb loin, about 2 pounds (ask your butcher to fan it out to a ¼-inch thickness)

KIMCHI PANCAKE
4 cups grated sweet potato
1 to 2 eggs, beaten
1 teaspoon minced Serrano pepper
1 tablespoon minced garlic
1 tablespoon minced fresh ginger
1 teaspoon chopped green onion
½ cup kimchi, finely chopped
½ cup rice flour, plus more as needed
Salt
Canola oil, for frying

SOY DRIZZLE
¼ cup soy sauce
2 tablespoons fresh lemon juice
2 tablespoons fish sauce

SUMAC YOGURT
1 cup plain whole-milk yogurt
1 teaspoon ground sumac
1 teaspoon ground cumin
1 teaspoon ground coriander
Salt and freshly ground black pepper, to taste

TO ASSEMBLE
Cilantro leaves
Green onions, chopped
White sesame seeds

To marinate the lamb: In a glass bowl or container, whisk together the green onions, chile, garlic, orange juice, mint, and olive oil until combined. Add the lamb and coat well. Cover and refrigerate overnight.

Heat a grill to medium-high.

Remove the lamb from the marinade and transfer to a platter—don't worry about patting dry. Over medium-high heat, grill on the first side for 4 minutes. Flip and grill for 3 minutes more to an internal temperature of 145°F for medium-rare. Transfer to a cutting board and allow to rest for at least 10 minutes.

To prepare the kimchi pancake: In a large bowl, mix the ingredients until a batter forms (start with 1 egg; you may not need both to bind your mixture, but add more as necessary). Using your hands, shape thin, flattened patties. In a medium sauté pan, warm enough canola oil over medium heat to cover the bottom of the pan. Cook 2 or 3 patties at a time for about 3 minutes on one side. Flip and cook until both sides are golden brown and cooked through. (Look for the potato to change color.) With a spatula, transfer each pancake to a rack and season with additional salt. (These can be prepared ahead of time and reheated in a 300°F oven as needed.)

To make the soy drizzle: In a small bowl, whisk together the soy sauce, lemon juice, and fish sauce until combined; set aside.

To make the sumac yogurt: In a small serving bowl, whisk all the ingredients together until well combined.

To assemble: Divide the hot pancakes among four plates. Slice the grilled lamb and top each pancake with the fanned slices. Top with the soy drizzle over the plates with a flurry of cilantro, sliced green onions, and sesame seeds. Serve immediately with the yogurt on the side.

Park's BBQ / Beef Bulgogi

At Park's BBQ, a time-honored and revered spot in the nation's largest Koreatown, Jenee Kim's extensive menu feels like an invitation to explore. Using Asian pear as a tenderizer, marinated and grilled "fire meat" bulgogi is your sesame-spiked gateway dish that hits spicy, salty, and sour in each bite. This recipe offers two foolproof ways to prepare bulgogi: in the oven or seared on the stovetop.

Along with rice, lettuce-wrapped bulgogi is enhanced with assortments of pickled and fermented *banchan* (think kimchi, seasoned soybeans, sweet-and-sour radish, chopped scallion pancakes) in tiny ramekins around the table. Korean barbecue is best enjoyed with friends, friends with kids, and friends who tote along Bandol rosé and Beaujolais.

SERVES 4

6 tablespoons soy sauce

¼ cup sugar

2 teaspoons honey

¼ cup sesame oil

¼ cup sake

1 teaspoon sesame seeds, lightly toasted

4 teaspoons finely minced garlic

¼ cup chopped green onion

¼ cup finely minced Asian pear

2 tablespoons finely minced white onion

Large pinch of freshly ground black pepper

2 pounds rib eye or sirloin steak, thinly sliced

Canola oil

Large lettuce leaves, for wrapping

In a large bowl, whisk together all the ingredients except the meat, canola oil, and lettuce leaves. Toss the meat with the marinade. Cover and refrigerate for 1 to 2 hours, tossing periodically.

To prepare the bulgogi in the oven: Preheat the oven to 375°F.

Remove the meat from the marinade and spread it in a single layer on a rimmed baking sheet. Roast for 10 to 12 minutes, rotating the pan halfway through, until the slices of beef are fully cooked and caramelized on the outside.

To sear the bulgogi on the stovetop: In a large cast-iron pan, lightly coat the bottom with canola oil and heat over high heat. Once the oil is hot but not smoking, add the beef to the pan. Sear until golden brown, jostling the pan and using tongs to turn every so often, 5 to 7 minutes, until the meat is caramelized and the exterior begins to crisp.

To assemble: Transfer the bulgogi meat to a platter and serve while hot with large lettuce leaves and Korean hot paste like *ssamjang*, or classic kimchi.

Everson Royce Bar / The Bar Burger

Humble and tasty, the Everson Royce Bar burger has no pretense to be anything other than a well-grilled quarter-pounder on a buttery domed bun. L.A.'s gladiatorial burger wars encourage a certain brand of showmanship, but for most home cooks, executing multiple impressive condiments just as often yields cold ingredients on a lukewarm patty. In contrast, Matt Molina's straightforward style tastes best straight off the grill or griddle, and because this classic version comes together quickly, it works.

MAKES 4

ERB DIJONNAISE
1½ cups canola oil
½ cup extra-virgin olive oil
2 egg yolks
2 teaspoons hot sauce
2 teaspoons Worcestershire sauce
1 tablespoon Dijon mustard
2 teaspoons fresh lemon juice
2 teaspoons very finely grated garlic
1 teaspoon (3 grams) Diamond Crystal kosher salt
Ice water, as needed

BURGER
1 pound prime ground chuck
Salt and freshly ground black pepper

TO ASSEMBLE
4 slices Tillamook cheddar
4 egg-brioche buns
Canola oil, for griddling
Dill pickle spears, for serving

To make the ERB Dijonnaise: In a measuring cup with a spout, combine the oils. In a food processor, combine the egg yolks, hot sauce, Worcestershire sauce, mustard, lemon juice, garlic, and salt. Process for 30 seconds. With the machine running, begin to pour in the oil, using the slowest steady stream you can manage. If oil begins to collect in the bowl at any time, stop streaming in the oil and allow the sauce to emulsify before adding more oil. If the Dijonnaise becomes too thick, add 1 tablespoon ice water to loosen. The desired consistency is rich and creamy, like a firm pudding, but not so stiff to form peaks. Transfer to an airtight container to chill. (The Dijonnaise will keep in the refrigerator for up to 1 week.)

To make the burger: Heat a grill or griddle. Cut a 6-inch square of waxed paper for each burger and line up the squares on a clean work surface.

Using a 4 ½-inch ring mold (or circles shaped out of foil), lightly shape even, flat patties from the ground beef on each square. Carefully unmold, and reshape if necessary. Season each well with salt and pepper. Stack the patties and paper for easy handling.

Lightly oil the griddle, then place the raw patties on the griddle, pressing down gently with the spatula so they sizzle lightly. After 3 minutes, flip and cook for 1 minute more before topping each patty with the cheddar. Griddle until the cheese starts to lose its opaqueness and the sides begin to wilt and collapse.

To assemble: Slice the brioche bun in half. Place both top and bottom, cut-sides down, on the griddle. Toast until they're crisp and almost fully browned. (There's enough butter in the brioche that they don't need any additional.) Using a spatula, remove to a plate or platter. Spread a heaping tablespoon of Dijonnaise over the bottom bun.

CONTINUED

The Bar Burger

Set one cheeseburger atop each Dijonnaise-smeared bun. Cap with the other half of the bun. Serve immediately with dill pickle spears as on the side.

MASTERING THE BAR BURGER:

- Grinding the beef fresh does make a difference; at Everson Royce Bar, Molina uses a custom blend ground from prime chuck and extra sirloin fat.

- As the meat cooks, escaping water can cause the patty to rise slightly in the middle, like a muffin. Molina encourages you to press down lightly with a spatula—the telltale sizzle is steam escaping.

- Look elsewhere for mile-high jawbreakers: Molina based this recipe off of the thinner-patty burgers of his youth like Jim's Burgers in the San Gabriel Valley.

- A good bun is a must. Don't skimp on the brioche.

BEYOND THE KALE
SALADS AND VEGETABLES

Baroo
Pineapple-Napa Cabbage Kimchi

Elf Café
Za'atar Caesar with Charred Hearts of Romaine and Crispy Capers

M Café de Chaya
M Chopped Salad with Tofu-Peppercorn Ranch

Jar
Creamed Spinach

Bäco Mercat
Melon & Herb Salad with Hazelnuts and Urfa Biber

Go Get Em Tiger
Grilled Panzanella with White Peach, Heirloom Tomato, and Fresh Cheese

n/naka
Classic Sunumono (Japanese Cucumber Salad)

Augustine Wine Bar
Falldorf Salad

Terrine Restaurant
Brussels Sprouts Salad with Pink Lady Apples, Pecorino, Spiced Pecans,
and Caramelized Shallot Dressing

Joan's On Third
Beets and Burrata with Baby Shiitake Mushrooms, Sugar Snap Peas, and Asparagus

Broken Spanish
Beet Pibil with Pickled Pearl Onions and Bitter Greens

Bar Moruno
Roasted Butternut Squash with Dukkah

Little Dom's
Cauliflower "Risotto"

Meals by Genet
Alitcha Kik (Yellow Split Pea Stew)

Trois Mec
Potato "Pulp" with Brown Butter, Bonito, and Onion Soubise

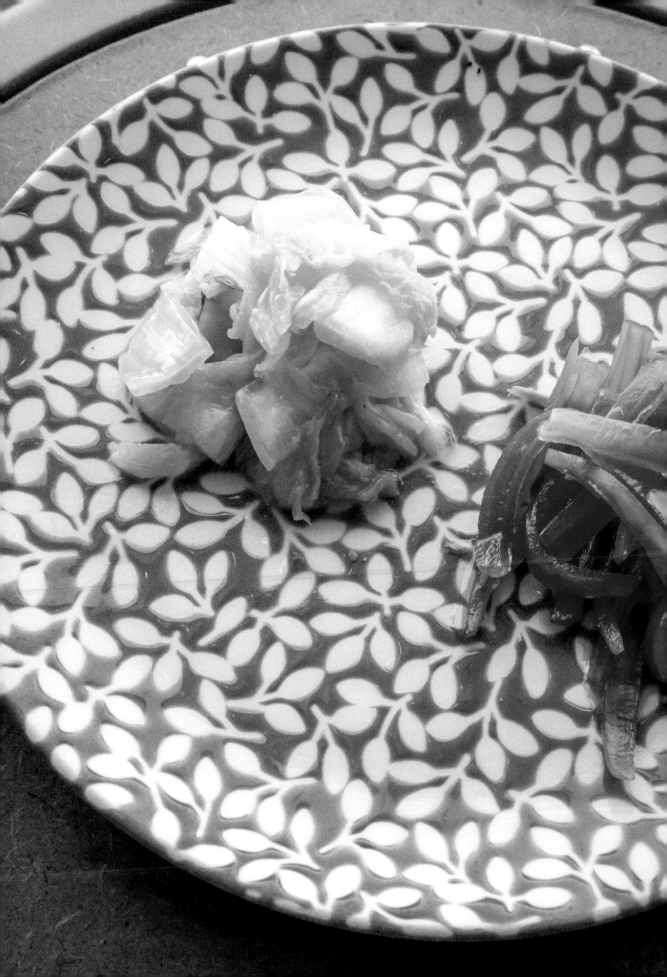

Baroo / Pineapple–Napa Cabbage Kimchi

Baroo practically hides on a nondescript stretch of East Hollywood, next to an even more anonymous set of storefronts. Inside, it's spare but warm. Jars of Sharpie-labeled fermenting curiosities await, courtesy of chef/co-owner Kwang Uh. A *baroo* is the vessel or bowl in which a Buddhist monk takes his or her meals, so imagine this pineapple-fermented Napa cabbage kimchi topping beautiful compositions like an L.A.-style kimchi fried rice. For digestion and flavor, grain bowls love a generous heaping. This one isn't spicy, so feel free to add Korean *gochugaru* if you'd like a little kick.

As for the world of lacto-fermentation crocks and containers, there's a world of pretty choice. Check the thrift shop before buying brand-new–many vintage sauerkraut jars come with two half-moon weights to keep the cabbage submerged. Air-lock fermentation isn't expensive and goes a long way to keeping your kitchen smelling rosy. Vacuum-sealed containers, which will lock out air as well as press down the cabbage, are available online or at Korean markets.

MAKES ABOUT 2 CUPS KIMCHI

1 pound (or 1 medium) firm Napa cabbage

1 tablespoon sea salt or Diamond Crystal kosher salt, or 3% weight of cabbage

1 cup fresh pineapple juice, or enough to submerge the cabbage

1⅗ ounces mother fermented juice, or 10% weight of cabbage (substitute pickling liquid or tepache), optional

Cut the cabbage into 1½-inch pieces. Rub it with the salt. Let sit in a large bowl until it softens and begins to release liquid, about 3 hours.

Squeeze out the cabbage, discarding the liquid. If it's too salty, give it a rinse. Transfer to a sterilized container. Strain in the pineapple juice, along with the optional mother fermented juice, to completely submerge the cabbage.

To ferment: Place the container at room temperature (about 75°F). As you check for souring development, you're looking for bubbles to be released from the liquid and a sour taste. This occurs usually within a week but is dependent on both kitchen temperature and humidity.

At Baroo, Kwang Uh recommends straining the fermented cabbage and allowing it to sit with fresh pineapple juice for a few hours before serving.

Elf Café / Za'atar Caesar with Charred Hearts of Romaine and Crispy Capers

In the not-too-distant past, opening a vegetarian bistro in Echo Park with only a few candlelit tables and a natural wine list was a gutsy move; but, Elf Café's bohemian flair continues to woo. I'm smitten with this warm weeknight salad of theirs that adapts easily for vegans. Delicate fried capers conjure the southern Mediterranean, while Urfa biber pepper (see page 185) lends exotic earthy dimension. And there's something about the salad-on-fire flirtiness of grilling romaine, treviso, escarole, and Little Gem. Wait until the last possible moment and lightly char as opposed to blackening the lettuce. The intense heat will wilt the leaves to limp, sad strips the longer it stays on the grill or cast-iron pan.

SERVES 4

½ cup mayonnaise

½ cup grated Parmesan

1 teaspoon chopped parsley

1 teaspoon plus 1 tablespoon za'atar

1 teaspoon fresh lemon juice

¼ cup heavy cream (optional)

Salt and cracked black or Urfa biber pepper

1 teaspoon nonpareil (brined) capers

Blended oil, for frying

6 pieces torn, rustic-style bread

2 heads romaine lettuce

1 tablespoon olive oil

2 radishes, thinly sliced

In a small bowl, whisk together the mayonnaise, Parmesan, parsley, 1 teaspoon of the za'atar, and the lemon juice. The consistency will be thick. (Loosen with up to ¼ cup cream, if desired.) Season with salt and pepper, and set aside.

Line a plate with paper towels. Pat the capers dry. (If they're salted, soak first for 15 minutes, then pat dry.) In a deep pot or cast-iron pan, heat about ¼ inch blended oil until shimmering. Being mindful of splattering as you add them, quick-fry the capers until they audibly pop and split open and become crispy, 45 seconds to 1 minute. Using a slotted spoon, transfer to the paper towels. While the oil is still hot, add the torn bread and fry until golden, turning as necessary. Using a slotted spoon or tongs, transfer the croutons to the paper towels. Season with salt and the remaining 1 tablespoon za'atar.

Right before serving, heat a grill or a large dry cast-iron pan. Cut the heads of romaine lengthwise and remove the hard part of the stem with a knife. (Don't remove the whole stem or the head will fall apart.) Rub the lettuce with the olive oil. Grill on both sides until lightly blackened but not too wilted, about 1 minute on each side.

Using tongs, transfer the charred lettuce to a serving platter, cut side up. Spoon the dressing on top. Top with the capers, croutons, and radishes, and finish with extra Parmesan and cracked black or Urfa biber pepper.

M Café de Chaya / M Chopped Salad with Tofu-Peppercorn Ranch

Maybe it's on account of La Scala Beverly Hills, or Nancy Silverton, but I can't help but free-associate L.A. and chopped salads. The dairy-free denizens of the world were beginning to miss their ranch dressing until they stepped under the lime-green umbrellas of the M Café patio. This silken tofu dressing for the macrobiotic restaurant's signature entrée salad is convincing, and versatile. And dill haters: I promise it's not overpowering but necessary to balance flavors. M Café chills its salad plates, much in the way you'd warm plates for pasta, to keep the lettuce extra crisp.

SERVES 4

TOFU-PEPPERCORN RANCH

¼ cup unsweetened rice milk

1½ tablespoons fresh lemon juice, plus more as needed

1 tablespoon apple cider vinegar

1 teaspoon umeboshi vinegar

1 small garlic clove, smashed

½ teaspoon minced tarragon

2 teaspoons minced dill

Pinch of dry mustard powder

½ teaspoon sea salt, plus more as needed

1 teaspoon coarsely ground black pepper

¾ cup Vegenaise

4 ounces silken tofu (about ½ package of the shelf-stable kind)

2 teaspoons sweet white miso

CHOPPED SALAD

8 cups mixed field greens

4 cups chopped romaine hearts

1 avocado, peeled, seeded, and flesh diced

1 medium cucumber, diced

1 cup drained cooked (or canned) chickpeas

2 green onions, sliced

1 carrot, shredded

1 small beet, shredded

4 radishes, quartered

½ cup prepared tempeh "bacon," cooked according to package directions and crumbled

1½ cups diced prepared marinated and baked tofu

Dill sprigs, for garnish

½ cup tamari-roasted or roasted and salted almonds

To make the dressing: In a blender, combine all the dressing ingredients and blend until smooth and creamy.

To assemble: Chill four large salad plates. In a bowl, combine all the lettuces and toss well with ½ to 1 cup of dressing. Pile onto the plates. Arrange the remaining ingredients on top, garnishing with dill sprigs and roasted almonds. Alternatively, the ingredients can be combined in a large bowl and tossed with the dressing family-style.

Jar / Creamed Spinach

Chef Suzanne Tracht's winning formula for L.A.'s stalwart modern steakhouse includes this rich and creamy spinach. The luxurious béchamel takes on the most inviting hue—it reminds one of pistachio or mint ice cream. As a tried-and-true side, creamed spinach is the best supporting actor to roasted meats, from a medium-rare New York Strip to Sonoma lamb. You hardly need more.

Chop the spinach according to your taste: finely for a more formal preparation; coarsely, if rustic is your gig. Try a final sprinkle of nutmeg. It was good enough for the spice traders to fight wars over, after all. Use any leftover béchamel to enhance casseroles or baked dishes.

SERVES 6

BÉCHAMEL

½ cup (1 stick) butter, cubed

½ onion, coarsely chopped

2 bay leaves

1 teaspoon whole black peppercorns

1 dried red chile

1 cup all-purpose flour

1 teaspoon table salt

4 cups milk

28 ounces (about 3 bags) fresh young spinach leaves, washed and trimmed

TO ASSEMBLE

2 cups heavy cream

2 teaspoons salt

2 teaspoons freshly ground black pepper

Freshly grated nutmeg, optional

To prepare the béchamel: In a heavy saucepan, warm the butter, onion, bay leaves, peppercorns, and dried chile over medium heat until the mixture is simmering. Add the flour and salt, whisking continuously, until the sauce comes together and is lightly browned and golden, about 10 minutes. Slowly whisk in the milk and increase the heat slightly. It will begin to thicken. Cook, stirring, until the béchamel is uniformly smooth.

Remove from the heat, pass the béchamel through a chinois or fine-mesh sieve, and set aside. (The béchamel can be refrigerated in an airtight container, then warmed over low heat.)

To blanch the spinach: Prepare an ice bath in the sink. Bring a large pot of aggressively salted water to a boil. Submerge the spinach in the boiling water for about 5 seconds, then immediately plunge into the ice bath to stop the cooking. When the leaves have cooled off, squeeze out all the water by hand or in a piece of cheesecloth. Transfer the spinach to a clean cutting board and chop.

To assemble: In a heavy saucepan, warm the cream, salt, and pepper over medium-low heat. When the mixture reaches a simmer, add ⅔ cup of the béchamel and whisk until combined. Add the spinach and a sprinkle of nutmeg and stir. Cook until fully heated through.

To serve: Transfer the creamed spinach to a serving dish and serve immediately. (The creamed spinach can be made a day in advance; store in refrigerator and reheat before serving.)

Bäco Mercat / Melon & Herb Salad with Hazelnuts and Urfa Biber

Urfa biber might sound like a hip baby name dreamed up by Silverlake millennials, but it's actually (or, more likely, also) a dried Turkish pepper. The crimson-black flecks, about the size of fleur de sel, bear faint flavor resemblance to Aleppo or chipotle pepper in complementing both sweet and savory preparations. Hardly surprising that Josef Centeno of Bäco Mercat would tap a global spice to complement a daring menu which already includes many peripheral to the U.S. *mise en place*, among them *mojama* (Spanish salt-cured tuna) and *abkhazian* spice (a potent chile-garlic herb condiment from the *other* Georgia).

For this summery salad, along with cooling mint and the refreshing crunch of bitter Belgian endive, the Urfa (also known as Isot pepper) provides a grounding counterpoint for the overeager sweetness of ripe melon. When picking through the melons, no matter the varietal, it's all about a firm rind, a fragrant aroma, and knocking for a hollow sound. (Those who follow Ayurvedic principles against combining dairy and melon can eliminate the yogurt in this recipe, no problem.)

SERVES 4

1 (2-pound) cantaloupe or Tuscan melon, peeled and cut into ⅛-inch-thick slices

2 heads Belgian endive, cored, trimmed, and leaves separated

½ cup parsley leaves, torn

½ cup mint leaves, torn

1 teaspoon sherry vinegar

¼ teaspoon (1½ grams) Diamond Crystal kosher salt

2½ tablespoons extra-virgin olive oil

Freshly ground black pepper

¼ cup plain yogurt

Pinch of flaky sea salt

¼ cup hazelnuts, lightly toasted and coarsely chopped

½ teaspoon Urfa biber pepper, plus more as needed

In a large bowl, gently mix the melon slices, endive, parsley, and mint. In a small bowl, whisk the vinegar and ⅛ teaspoon of the kosher salt until the salt has dissolved. Add 1 tablespoon of the olive oil and a few grinds of black pepper. Whisk until well combined. Pour this over the melon and herb salad. Add the remaining ⅛ teaspoon kosher salt and toss gently.

In a small bowl, whisk the remaining olive oil with the yogurt, flaky sea salt, and a few grinds of black pepper until well combined.

To serve: Drizzle the yogurt dressing on top, and sprinkle with the hazelnuts and the Urfa biber. Serve while crisp.

Go Get Em Tiger / Grilled Panzanella with White Peach, Heirloom Tomato, and Fresh Cheese

Go Get Em Tiger continued on the path of L.A.'s coffee evolution, courtesy of Intelligentsia alums Kyle Glanville and Charles Babinski (G&B Coffee). Their concept stores in Larchmont Village and Los Feliz are complete with a killer brunch menu, including this sultry summer salad that zings with peak-season stone fruit. You get the pow! of a sherry vinaigrette, heirloom tomatoes, and dreamy ricotta or burrata. Well suited for a housewarming or picnic, the panzanella will keep for four hours at room temperature. Maximize this freshness by prepping the croutons at the last possible moment you can, making certain the bread is thoroughly dried and toasted in the oven before assembling the salad, and dress the salad after you've arrived at your destination.

Za'atar comes in green and red varieties, and the one used in this panzanella offers fragrant floral notes and a mild citrus tartness. The red mix used by Rosanna (Rosy) Huang, who created this recipe for a GGET pop-up, also has sesame, thyme, anise, and salt. Huang recommends dark, rich Chocolate Stripe tomatoes and Japanese heirlooms, if you can find them.

SERVES 4 TO 6

⅓ pound country bread, preferably day-old, sliced 1 inch thick

6 to 8 tablespoons extra-virgin olive oil

Diamond Crystal kosher salt

2 tablespoons sherry vinegar (preferably Pedro Ximénez)

Zest of 1 lemon

2 tablespoons fresh lemon juice

Salt and freshly ground black pepper

1 pound ripe heirloom tomatoes, cut into ¼-inch wedges

1 pound ripe white peaches (or similar stone fruit), cut into ¼-inch wedges

1 pound burrata, cut or torn into 1-inch pieces, or ricotta

1 teaspoon za'atar

2 teaspoons bite-size basil and/or opal basil leaves

Maldon sea salt

To grill the bread: Heat a grill or cast-iron pan. Brush the bread slices with 2 tablespoons of the olive oil. Place on the hot grill, and let sit undisturbed until the edges are slightly charred and toasted. Using tongs or a spatula, flip, and char the second side. When both sides are charred and golden, transfer to a cutting board. Sprinkle both sides with salt. Allow the toasts to cool enough to slice into 1-inch cubes.

To make the vinaigrette: Using a whisk, in a small bowl, emulsify the 6 remaining tablespoons olive oil, with the vinegar, lemon zest, and lemon juice. Season and set aside.

To assemble: In a large bowl, gently toss the tomatoes and white peaches with half the vinaigrette. Add the toasted bread cubes and toss, drizzling with additional vinaigrette until the salad is coated but not soggy. Arrange the panzanella on a large platter or shallow bowl. Dab mounds of cheese on top. Garnish with za'atar and scatter the basil leaves over the top. To finish, a pinch of Maldon sea salt should do. (Optionally, a last drizzle of olive oil on top really gives the salad a beautiful shine.)

n/naka / Classic Sunumono (Japanese Cucumber Salad)

Chef Niki Nakayama says the best thing about Japanese cookery is that so much of it is ratio-based. Her recipe for traditional cucumber salad—part of a multicourse *kaiseki* tasting filled with produce she farms herself—includes a simple ratio referred to as *san bai zu*, "3 cups of vinegar." While you can halve this recipe with plenty to go around, it's only fitting to give the recipe for 3 cups, so save n/naka's leftovers in the fridge. Add onion, ginger, or garlic for different quick pickles, or mix it with flavored oil as a dressing or marinade. Substitute bouillon-like dashi powder if you want to skip simmering the bonito with leathery strips of dried kombu seaweed. That substance on kombu's surface is crystallized glutamate (not dust or mold), a powerful source of umami.

MAKES 3 CUPS *SAN BAI ZU*

¾ ounce kombu (1 ounce if vegetarian)

6 cups water

¾ ounce bonito flakes (skip for vegetarian)

3 cups rice vinegar

1 cup sugar

1 cup light soy sauce

1 teaspoon salt, plus more as needed

TO ASSEMBLE

Persian or hothouse cucumbers

Ice water

Edible flowers

Sesame seeds, for garnish

To make the dashi stock: In a large stockpot, soak the kombu in the water for at least 30 minutes. It will soften and become more pliable, and the water will begin to brine. Place the stockpot over medium-high heat and bring to a boil. Reduce to a faint simmer and cook for 10 minutes. Taste as you go—the flavor should stay subtle but increase in umami.

Turn off the heat if you will be adding bonito; continue to simmer for 20 additional minutes if you are making a vegan (kombu-only) dashi. To continue, add a splash of cool water and add the bonito. Allow the flakes to steep for 10 minutes. Strain the broth through a mesh sieve and reserve. (You can also soak the kombu at room temperature overnight. The dashi stock will freeze well or keep in the refrigerator for a few days.)

To make the *san bai zu*: Combine 5 cups of the dashi stock, the vinegar, sugar, light soy sauce, and salt in a large stockpot and bring to a simmer. As soon as it comes to a simmer and the sugar has dissolved, turn off the heat and transfer the vinegar to an airtight container to chill in the refrigerator, where it will keep for about a month. Chilling the vinegar right away, instead of letting it cool, helps preserve the flavor.

Using a mandoline, thinly slice cucumbers into a bowl. Salt the slices aggressively, and using your hands mix and mash the cucumber together to soften. Rinse immediately with ice water, making sure to squeeze out the water from the cucumbers. The cucumbers should be soft.

To assemble one serving: Place a small mound of thin-sliced cucumber (about half of one cucumber or ¼ cup slices) in a serving bowl and pour over the chilled vinegar mixture from the side. Garnish with edible flowers and sesame seeds.

Augustine Wine Bar / Falldorf Salad

Faithful to its name, this salad from Studio City's food-forward Augustine Wine Bar delivers on autumnal colors. Persimmon runs the tables at the farmers' market come November, so pair the bright orange fruit with burnished candied pecans, deep green arugula and herbs, purple grapes, sliced red apples, and blue Gorgonzola. Flavor-wise, the tangy-sweet cheese in particular stands out against a vinaigrette of pickled fennel brine and shoyu. Not exactly the mayo-blanketed Waldorf salad of 1950s hotel luncheon lore.

The salad does well passed around the Thanksgiving table, or you can build it into an entrée by marinating a chicken breast with some of the dressing and grilling it, then slicing the meat. The pickled fennel, which doesn't end up in the salad but certainly could as a stand-in to a Waldorf's celery, is a versatile, refreshing condiment anywhere you'd use pickled onions. Sprinkle them on burgers, tacos, roasted fish, or avocado toast.

SERVES 4

CANDIED PECANS
2 egg whites
¼ cup sugar
1½ teaspoons water
¼ teaspoon ground fennel seeds
¼ teaspoon ground cinnamon
½ pound raw pecans
Salt

WHITE SOY-FENNEL VINAIGRETTE
1 fennel bulb
1 cup plus 2 tablespoons water
7 tablespoons rice vinegar, divided
6 tablespoons sugar
3 tablespoons salt
½ cup shoyu (white soy sauce)
2 tablespoons yuzu juice
1 tablespoon aged balsamic vinegar
2 cups extra-virgin olive oil

TO ASSEMBLE
2 large handfuls of wild arugula
1 Fuyu persimmon, cut into slices
1 cup seedless grapes, halved
1 Honeycrisp apple, sliced
1 tablespoon chopped mixed herbs, such as parsley, chives, tarragon, and chervil
½ cup crumbled Gorgonzola cheese

To candy the pecans: Preheat the oven to 250°F. Butter a rimmed baking sheet.

In a bowl, whisk the egg whites, sugar, water, ground fennel, and cinnamon until foamy. Add the pecans and toss until well coated. Season with salt. Spread the nuts evenly on a baking sheet and roast, stirring every 15 minutes. When sufficiently dried and caramelized, remove from the oven and let cool on the sheet.

To make the vinaigrette: First, slice the fennel into slivers and pack into a small jar.

In a pot, combine the water, 6 tablespoons rice vinegar, sugar, and salt and stir. Heat over medium heat. Once the sugar and salt are fully dissolved and the mixture is boiling to the point where it will still bubble after you stir it, pour it over the sliced fennel. Cover and allow to cool. Once the jar is at room temperature, place in the refrigerator to pickle. To quick pickle, leave overnight, or for up to 5 days. (Reserve the pickled fennel for other use.)

To finish the vinaigrette: In a bowl, whisk together ¾ cup of the pickling liquid with the shoyu, yuzu juice, balsamic vinegar, and remaining 1 tablespoon rice vinegar. Whisk in the olive oil, taste, and adjust the seasoning.

To serve: In a large bowl, combine the arugula, persimmon, grapes, and apple slices. Add the herbs and toss with about half the vinaigrette (enough to coat but not saturate the salad). Top with the Gorgonzola cheese and candied pecans, and serve immediately.

Terrine Restaurant / Brussels Sprouts Salad with Pink Lady Apples, Pecorino, Spiced Pecans, and Caramelized Shallot Dressing

During the bacon frenzy of the early 2010s, there was a moment when you couldn't swing a baguette without hitting a gastropub roasting its Brussels sprouts with some variant of pig. Like a cover band butchering "Stairway to Heaven," no one ever seemed to rock it quite right. Chefs soon discovered it was best to move into shreds and slaws, raw and grilling on the stalk—and the errant Thanksgiving centerpiece. At Terrine, French classics, charcuteries, and velvety pâtés illuminate the menu because Kris Morningstar is a master of textures.

The brasserie's unsung hero is a seasonal array of crisp shredded sprouts against harvest-rich flavors like sweet dates and candied pecans, bright Pink Lady apples, and a nutty pecorino. The hidden complexity, though, comes from a soulful caramelized shallot vinaigrette. As you're sautéing, remember to keep the fragrant shallots in the center of the pan so the little bits don't burn.

SERVES 4 TO 6

CARAMELIZED SHALLOT DRESSING

1 cup plus 1 tablespoon canola oil

1½ large shallots, thinly sliced (generous ½ cup)

¾ cup white balsamic vinegar

¼ teaspoon Dijon mustard

Salt

TO ASSEMBLE

½ cup sugar

½ cup water

3 ounces whole pecans

Salt

Canola oil, for frying

1 pound Brussels sprouts, shaved

4 ounces dates, pitted and sliced into rings

1 Pink Lady apple, cubed

4 ounces Pecorino Toscana, cubed

To make the dressing: In a sauté pan, heat 1 tablespoon of the canola oil over high heat and cook the shallots until lightly caramelized, stirring often, about 6 minutes. When the color is dark golden, add the vinegar and allow the liquid to reduce by half, about 2 minutes. Transfer this mixture to a blender and puree. Stop the machine and add the mustard, the remaining 1 cup of canola oil, and salt. Puree again until smooth, scraping down the sides as necessary, and set aside.

To candy the pecans: Set a rack over a baking sheet lined with parchment. In a small saucepan, bring the sugar and water to a boil. Add the pecans and simmer until the sugar dissolves, 2 to 3 minutes. Remove from the heat and allow the pecans and liquid to cool together.

In a cast-iron pan, heat about 2 inches of oil over medium-low heat to 280°F. Slowly add the pecans and fry for 6 minutes, or until a cascade of bubbles forms around the pecans (as if it's foaming at the mouth). Transfer the pecans to the rack as you go. They should be a little syrupy/sticky. Add a tiny pinch of salt. (The nuts will keep in an airtight container for at least a month.)

To assemble: In a large bowl, toss the shaved Brussels sprouts with the dates, apple, Pecorino, pecans, and a generous ¾ cup of the dressing. Add more until the salad is well coated. Season to taste and serve.

Joan's On Third / Beets and Burrata with Baby Shiitake Mushrooms, Sugar Snap Peas, and Asparagus

This place is not just "Some lady's on Third." It's *Joan's*. No shadowy Oz behind the curtain, Joan McNamara, L.A.'s grande dame of grab-and-go, is usually around in a black logo'd apron and never without a smile. Since 1995, her well-merchandised market, straight out of central casting, has been ground zero for people-watching on the patio and loading up a handheld basket with twine-tied ficelles, Chinese chicken salads, and Joan's iconic brownies for Hollywood Bowl picnicking. Though burrata is fragile and tastes best within a day of purchase, this bright spring salad travels just as well as goat cheese salads and capreses.

SERVES 4

½ bunch asparagus spears

Sugar snap peas, halved on the diagonal

1 bunch baby golden or Chioggia (candy-stripe) beets

8 baby or 5 regular shiitake mushrooms, cleaned

3 tablespoons olive oil

Salt and freshly ground black pepper

8 ounces burrata, sliced

3 tablespoons aged balsamic vinegar

4 ounces microgreens or arugula

Set a bowl of ice and water in the sink, fitted with a colander. Fill a stockpot with salted water and bring to a boil. Add the asparagus and blanch for 30 seconds. Using a strainer, quickly remove and plunge into the ice bath. Pat dry with a paper towel, and slice into 1½-inch segments.

Repeat the blanching process with the sugar snap peas. Transfer the snap peas and asparagus to a large bowl and set aside. Do not discard the boiling water.

Add the beets to the pot, and boil until fork-tender. While the beets are boiling, remove the stems from the mushrooms. Remove the beets and transfer to a clean cutting surface to cool, then peel and slice.

In a sauté pan, warm 1 tablespoon of the olive oil over medium heat. Add the mushrooms, and allow them to sit undisturbed for 1 to 2 minutes, as they soften and release some of their liquid before stirring. Sauté until tender, stirring occasionally, another 2 to 3 minutes. Transfer to the bowl and toss with the asparagus and sugar snap peas. Add the remaining 2 tablespoons olive oil, and season with salt and pepper.

To assemble the salad: Place slices of burrata on a platter. Scatter beet slices over the cheese, then top with the vegetable mixture. Drizzle the vinegar over the top, and garnish with microgreens.

Broken Spanish / Beet Pibil with Pickled Pearl Onions and Bitter Greens

Cochinita pibil gets a smoky beet overhaul in this modern Mexican pork switcharoo. Both at Broken Spanish and B.S. Taqueria, Ray Garcia showers equal love on whole animal cuts and foraged or farmers' market vegetables. The time-honored dish retains its soulfulness with a tangy, earthy marinade, bites of caramelized "meat," and telltale achiote hue. The fuchsia pop of its one-day onion pickle will call out from the corner reaches of the refrigerator. It adds sweet-hot punch to everything from takeout tacos to rich stews to avocado toasts. A warning: Annatto is a powerful colorant much like turmeric, so avoid using white pots or white plastic. The stains will fade, but on island time.

SERVES 6 TO 8

PICKLED PEARL ONIONS

20 red pearl onions, peeled

2 cups red wine vinegar

3 habañero chiles (depending on your tolerance), stemmed

BEET PIBIL

24 yellow beets, golf ball size

3 tablespoons achiote (annatto seed)

1½ tablespoons dried Mexican oregano

1 teaspoon cumin seed

½ teaspoon ground allspice

½ teaspoon whole black peppercorns

1 tablespoon vegetable oil, plus more as needed

2 cups water

1 cup coconut vinegar

½ cup distilled white vinegar

½ cup fresh orange juice

Salt

2 medium white onions, quartered

2 habañero chiles (or fewer, depending on your tolerance), stemmed

Bitter greens, such as kale, mustard greens, mustard frills, or arugula, for garnish

To pickle the onions: Pack the pearl onions into a clean, dry jar. In a pot, stir together the vinegar and habañeros. Bring to a boil over medium heat, then pour the liquid over the onions. Cover and let cool to room temperature. Refrigerate for 24 hours.

To prepare the beets: Using a scouring pad, scrub the beets to remove the outer layer of dirt/skin.

In a spice grinder or molcajete, combine the achiote, oregano, cumin, allspice, and peppercorns. Grind until relatively smooth.

In a 4-quart pot, add enough vegetable oil as needed for a thin layer, and heat over medium heat. Once hot but not smoking, add the ground spices. Stirring continuously, cook for about 2 minutes, until the aromatics are released. Add the water, coconut vinegar, distilled vinegar, and orange juice, and stir.

Bring the mixture to a simmer, then remove from the heat, season with salt, and let cool.

To cook the beets: Transfer the cooled liquid to a separate large pot, along with the quartered onions, stemmed chiles, and beets. Cover the pot tightly with foil to help trap the steam, and secure the lid on top of the foil. Cook the beets over low heat for 2 to 3 hours, stirring halfway through. You are looking for beets that are fork tender and fully cooked through. When ready, remove the beets to a bowl or plate and allow them to cool. Do not discard the cooking liquid.

In a blender, combine the remaining liquid, the onions, habañeros, and 3 of the beets. Puree until smooth. Pass through a fine strainer and set aside.

Preheat the oven to 400°F. Rub the beets lightly in vegetable oil and arrange on a baking sheet. Sprinkle with salt. Roast the beets until deeply caramelized and darkened on the tips, about 12 minutes.

To assemble: Serve the roasted beets hot with the pibil sauce, pickled red pearl onions, and bitter greens.

Bar Moruno / Roasted Butternut Squash with Dukkah

Truth be told, the first time I made dukkah at home, I ate most of the chunky spice blend like a snack mix. Happily, this recipe makes enough extra to snack on. Egyptian-origin dukkah is usually a toasted blend of nuts and earthy spices such as cumin and coriander. Chris Feldmeier at Moruno downtown draws out the natural honey flavors of butternut squash for a gorgeous, nutty, roasted vegetable side that's basically a culinary archetype for autumn.

For its delicious versatility, dukkah should easily claim ongoing space in your pantry. Use it as a stand-in for bread crumbs to crust chicken, fish, or fresh chèvre; sprinkle it over eggs. When guests suddenly show up, swirl it into sour cream for an instant dip and grab some lavash, or dust it over almond milk ricotta with a few healthy glugs of good-quality olive oil.

SERVES 4

1½ cups raw cashews

1 tablespoon whole cumin seeds

2 tablespoons whole coriander seeds

⅓ cup sesame seeds

1 tablespoon nigella seeds (*kalonji*)

½ cup (1 stick) butter, room temperature

1½ teaspoons Aleppo pepper

Salt

1 whole butternut squash

2 tablespoons honey

To prepare the dukkah: Preheat the oven to 325°F. Spread the cashews on a rimmed baking sheet and toast for 8 to 10 minutes, until they smell nutty and are just turning golden. Keep an eye on them!

Transfer the toasted nuts to a cutting board and coarsely chop while warm. Roughly grind or crush the cumin and coriander.

Separately, in a small saucepan, toast the sesame and nigella seeds over high heat until fragrant and the white seeds just begin to show color. Don't let them brown or they'll burn before you scoop them out of the skillet. Set the seeds aside to cool.

Wipe out the saucepan with a paper towel. Over medium heat, melt 4 tablespoons of the butter. It will begin to bubble and foam, and when it begins to brown and smell nutty, add the crushed cumin and coriander, and cook in the butter for up to 2 minutes (lower the heat if the spices begin to pop). Stir in the chopped cashews and cook for another 1 to 2 minutes, stirring so the nuts do not burn. Add the sesame seeds, nigella seeds, and Aleppo pepper and stir until well combined. Remove from the heat, season with salt, and transfer the finished dukkah to a small bowl. Keep the dukkah in the refrigerator in an airtight container for up to a month.

Increase the oven temperature to 350°F. Split the butternut squash lengthwise and remove the seeds. Using a sharp knife, score the thick end deeply. Salt and rub each squash half with the remaining 4 tablespoons butter. Cover the flesh with the honey, then a generous amount of the dukkah. Place on a rimmed baking sheet and roast for 30 minutes, or until the squash is cooked enough to have some give, but not shriveled. Be mindful so the cashews do not burn or blacken.

Remove from the oven and allow the squash to cool briefly before transferring to a platter. Scoop up any dukkah that has fallen onto the baking sheet. Serve immediately.

Little Dom's / Cauliflower "Risotto"

Chef Brandon Boudet of Little Dom's developed this "risotto" with the idea of making a guilty pleasure a little more guilt-free. There's no grain or rice in the risotto; the cauliflower is shaved down and cooked in the same way as a risotto would be. Given the recent proliferation of bagged pre-riced cauliflower on the market, from Whole Foods to Trader Joe's, the dish can fold into your routine as a go-to on weeknights when you want a fast indulgence.

Chef Boudet recommends a light red wine to pair with the earthy flavor of the cauliflower. Leftovers will work really well with oven-roasted eggs and romesco sauce (page 102), or mixed with eggs and spinach and fried up like rice arancini.

SERVES 4

1 head cauliflower
6 tablespoons (¾ stick) butter
¼ cup olive oil
4 green onions, finely chopped
¾ teaspoon red pepper flakes
Salt
1¼ cups (about 4 ounces) grated Parmesan

Using the large holes of a grater or shredder attachment of a food processor, grate the cauliflower.

In a regular sauté pan, melt the butter in the olive oil over medium-low heat. Add the green onions, red pepper flakes, and salt. Sweat, stirring, but do not brown the onions. Add the cauliflower and continue to sweat, stirring continuously. (Again, do not brown the vegetables.) You want to steam the vegetables to resemble rice as much as possible. Add a few tablespoons of water so there's a little bit of steam coming off the pan, keeping the heat at a lower temperature, and stir occasionally.

Once the cauliflower is just tender, turn off the heat and fold in the grated Parmesan, stirring constantly to thoroughly incorporate and melt the cheese.

To assemble: Transfer the risotto to a platter while hot.

Meals by Genet / Alitcha Kik (Yellow Split Pea Stew)

Ground zero at night for family celebrations and awkward first dates, Meals by Genet holds only 20 tables, and its infectiously sweet owner is the unspoken queen of Little Ethiopia's microcosm. Genet Agonafer loves to spread the love, and much of it to critic and true champion Jonathan Gold, who included Genet, and her two-day chicken *dorowot*, in his documentary.

Impossibly, she's a self-taught cook, giving hope to the rest of us. She learned by watching at the side of the woman who raised her mother. This is a dish you can make more on the fly than lentils, because split peas are grown to be dried and don't require presoaking. This yellow split pea stew is terrific for kids—her granddaughter, Ria, adores it—because it's mellow (*alitcha* means "not spicy"). She has no qualms spooning in extra garlic and salt, though. The stiff paste makes a killer falafel-like fritter, too (see page 160). Wrap them up Madcapra-style with griddled flatbread, tons of vinegary pickled and fresh veggies, and tahini sauce.

SERVES 4 TO 6

1 pound dried yellow split peas
5 white onions
3 tablespoons vegetable oil
2½ tablespoons minced garlic
2 teaspoons ground turmeric
Salt
Injera, for serving (optional)

First, pick through the split peas and discard any green or brown ones.

Put the split peas in a medium stockpot and cover them with enough water to double the height. Do not add salt. Bring to a simmer then cook the split peas over medium-low heat, uncovered, until soft and toothy, not too mushy, 45 to 60 minutes. Set aside.

In a large pot of unsalted water, boil the onions until very soft, about 45 minutes. Drain and transfer the onions to a blender or food processor, and puree until smooth. Place 2 cups of the onion puree back in the pot over medium heat. Before it begins to bubble, add the vegetable oil and garlic and gently sweat the onions and garlic, stirring continuously. Cook them until translucent but not browned, 5 to 10 minutes. Sprinkle in the turmeric and stir in the cooked split peas. The mixture should come to a strong boil. Season with salt as the mixture cooks down. Stir occasionally, adding splashes of water if the split peas begin to dry out, 30 to 45 minutes. It should be bright yellow, a little stiff, but not too dry or gritty, much like the texture of cottage cheese.

To serve: Transfer the hot or room-temperature stew to a serving bowl. Serve alongside *injera*, or as an accompaniment to meats and other vegetable dishes.

Trois Mec / Potato "Pulp" with Brown Butter, Bonito, and Onion Soubise

Opening in a Hollywood strip mall in 2013 (look for the Rafallo's pizza sign) as the combined vision of Ludo Lefevbre (Ludobites) and Jon Shook and Vinny Dotolo (Animal, Son of a Gun, Jon & Vinny's), Trois Mec quickly became the center of a new wave dining empire.

In this deconstructed and reconstructed answer to fondue-like mashed potato dish *pommes aligot*, what looks like shredded potato with pencil shavings is not so! The now-iconic potato pulp layers dense onion soubise, riced potato, Salers cheese, and a hit of umami-rich bonito flakes and brown butter done two ways. Salers can be a challenge to find, so keep an eye out for comparable Cantal.

SERVES 4 TO 6

10 to 12 French fingerling potatoes

2 ounces Salers cheese

BROWN BUTTER

2 cups (4 sticks) European-style unsalted butter, such as Plugra

ONION SOUBISE

4⅓ pounds white onions, cut into julienne

2 cups (4 sticks) butter

1½ cups heavy cream

⅛ teaspoon fleur de sel

BROWN BUTTER POWDER

1⅛ cups (75 grams) nonfat dry milk powder

½ cup clarified butter (see page 82)

¾ teaspoon sea salt

30 grams maltodextrin (see Note)

TO ASSEMBLE

6 grams bonito, freshly shaved or flaked

1½ teaspoons fleur de sel

1¼ teaspoons ground white pepper

To prepare the potatoes: Fill a large stockpot with water. Wash and scrub the potatoes, then add them to the pot and bring to a boil. Cook for 10 to 15 minutes, until the potatoes are fork-tender. Drain the potatoes and set aside to cool slightly. While still warm, peel each potato with a small paring knife and set aside.

To make the brown butter: Begin by fitting a chinois or strainer over a small bowl nested in a larger bowl filled with ice and water. In a saucepan, melt the butter over medium heat. Once melted, whisk continuously, swirling the pan as the butter begins to foam up, until the butter begins to change color and darkens to a golden brown, 9 to 10 minutes. The smell should be fragrant and nutty. Immediately strain into the bowl set in the ice bath, without wetting the butter. (When you are ready to use the butter, you'll put it in another saucepan to reheat.)

To make the onion soubise: In a medium saucepan, melt the butter over medium heat. Add the onions and gently sweat until soft, stirring occasionally, about 10 minutes, making sure not to brown them. Reduce the heat if you hear sizzling. Add the cream and cook gently over medium-low heat for 45 minutes, stirring every few minutes. Strain the onions and transfer to a blender, but reserve the cooking liquid. Puree the onions, and with the machine running, slowly add in enough of the reserved cooking liquid to reach the consistency of a smooth, dense puree—thick but not pasty. (You may not need all the liquid.) Stir in the fleur de sel.

To make the brown butter powder: In a blender, puree the milk powder, clarified butter, and salt until smooth. Let cool. Put the maltodextrin in a bowl and incorporate the mixture, mixing well with your hands. Pass this through a chinois or tammis.

CONTINUED

Potato "Pulp" with Brown Butter, Bonito, and Onion Soubise
CONTINUED

To assemble one portion: Set a ricer to a medium-size hole, about the width of an udon noodle. Spoon a dollop of the warmed onion soubise onto a plate. Pass 2 peeled potatoes through the ricer directly over the plate. Spoon 2 tablespoons of hot brown butter on top of the potatoes. Sprinkle generously with fleur du sel and white pepper. Grate enough cheese on top to cover the potatoes. Finish with a confetti of bonito and 1 to 2 tablespoons of brown butter powder. Serve immediately.

Note: As far as textural alchemy is concerned, ethereal powders that turn to oil in your mouth with an intense concentration of flavor is possible thanks to maltodextrin, a starch-derived additive that you can find at Surfas or online. Mind you, brown butter powder won't last unless you vacuum seal it, so it's best to make only what you need for the recipe.

SWEET SPOT

DESSERTS AND CONFECTIONS

McCall's Meat and Fish Co.
Strawberry Pâtes de Fruit

Paloma's Paletas
The Paloma

Alma
Frozen Yogurt with Whipped Celery Root Mousse and Passion Fruit

Proof Bakery
Flourless Chocolate Cake

Spago Beverly Hills
Almond-Ginger Cake with Crème Fraîche Whipped Cream
and Tangerine-Yuzu Reduction

Little Flower Candy Co.
Olive Oil Cake with Brown Butter Frosting

Jon & Vinny's
Rosemary-Pine Nut Tart

Rucker's Pies
Berry Lattice Pie

Pizzeria Mozza
Meyer Lemon Gelato Pie
with Champagne Vinegar Sauce and Candied Lemon Zest

Valerie Confections
"Fallen Fruit" Cake

Bottega Louie
Butterscotch Budino with Caramel Sauce

Church & State
Pots de Crème au Chocolat

The Sycamore Kitchen
Salted Chocolate Chip Rye Cookies

McCall's Meat and Fish Co. / Strawberry Pâtes de Fruit

Seems illogical for the city's most boutique butcher and fishmonger to offer a pastry case next to the meat, but husband-and-wife chef-owners Nathan McCall and Karen Yoo's pastry roots run deep. When tied up in boxes with grosgrain ribbon, these sugar-rolled pâtes de fruit make ideal hostess gifts. Note that strawberry contains a lower concentration of natural pectin than orchard fruits such as pear, apple, or citrus. If you decide to experiment, reference a pectin chart to get the right ratio. For consistency, Chef Yoo recommends purchased fruit puree, such as Boiron, available online. Enjoy admirable, if less refined, results from pureed-and-strained frozen berries. Check the bulk herbs aisle for citric acid by the pound, so you don't have to buy a jug of it. A digital scale makes the precise amounts called for in candy-making a breeze.

MAKES ONE 13 X 18-INCH SHEET OF ½- TO ¾-INCH-THICK CANDIES

60 grams pectin
1,100 grams sugar
18 grams citric acid
423 grams water
1,000 grams strawberry puree
200 grams lemon juice, strained
900 grams glucose
Granulated or crystallized sugar, for rolling

Grease a 13 x 18-inch rimmed baking sheet lightly with nonstick cooking spray or oil and line it with parchment paper.

Set out two bowls. In the first bowl, whisk together the pectin and 100 grams of the sugar. In the second bowl, combine the citric acid and 18 grams of the water. Set both bowls and the baking sheet near the stove.

Affix a candy thermometer to the side of a large saucepan. Put the strawberry puree, lemon juice, remaining 1,000 grams sugar, remaining 405 grams water, and glucose. Cook over high heat, whisking as you go. The lumps will dissolve as the mixture heats, and when it just comes to a boil, slowly sprinkle in the pectin-sugar mixture, whisking continuously. Cook, stirring occasionally to prevent the bottom from sticking and burning, until the mixture registers 221°F. As soon as you hit this temperature, quickly whisk in the citric acid–water mixture. Immediately pour the liquid into the baking sheet and set aside to cool, undisturbed.

To cut the candies, sprinkle a light layer of sugar over the top of the set pâtes de fruit. Run a paring knife around the edge of the pan to release the sides. Turn it out onto a clean cutting surface, sugared-side down. Peel off the parchment paper. Grease a sharp knife with a small amount of nonstick spray or oil. Slice the block into your desired squares or tiles, wiping the knife clean after every few cuts. The candy will be quite sticky. Roll the cut pieces in sugar for presentation. The pâtes de fruit will keep at room temperature in a parchment-lined airtight container for up to 1 month.

Paloma's Paletas / The Paloma

The paloma, that quintessential Mexican combination of grapefruit soda, lime, and tequila, rivals maybe horchata and micheladas in the realm of name-checked Angeleno drinks. From a fresh paleta company comes one that's, well, cooler. Edible flowers are suspended in this adorable grapefruit-lime pop. When served at sunset with tiny shots of tequila, you'll forget all about June gloom.

No molds on hand? Option A: Fill small tumblers, cover with foil, and poke a short skewer or stick in them. Option B: Make a granita. Pour the paleta mixture into a shallow glass or metal baking dish and freeze for 4 hours. Be diligent. Set a timer to give a thorough stir and scrape down the sides every 30 minutes, so ice crystals don't clump and the consistency remains smooth. The B version will keep for about a day.

MAKES 6 PALETAS

1½ cups (300 grams) water
½ cup (100 grams) sugar
1 pint (450 grams) grapefruit juice
Juice of 3½ limes (70 grams)
½ cup edible micro flowers

In a small pot, combine ½ cup of the water and the sugar, and warm over medium heat until the sugar has completely dissolved. When the mixture just reaches a simmer, remove it from the heat, transfer to a bowl, and chill.

If you're squeezing your own fruits, here's your moment. In a large bowl, combine the grapefruit and lime juices (using a strainer to catch seeds will help), fully cooled simple syrup, and remaining 1 cup water. Stir to combine.

Prepare 3-ounce molds by sprinkling 2 teaspoons of edible flowers into each. Top off with the juice blend. Carefully place in the freezer, with ice pop sticks in the mold. Freeze until solid, at least 4 to 6 hours. When ready to serve, dip the molds (very) briefly in hot water to release the pops.

Alma / Frozen Yogurt with Whipped Celery Root Mousse and Passion Fruit

When Alma opened as a pop-up inspired by Southern California terroir in 2012, the food scene embraced its creativity, its playfulness, and especially its seaweed beignets. Chef Ari Taymor and General Manager Ashleigh Parsons collected accolades, including 2013's Best New Restaurant from *Bon Appétit*. Today, in permanent residency at the Standard Hotel, Alma continues to push the envelope while staying active in the community, teaching school kids how to cook at its farm in Silverlake.

In L.A., the frozen yogurt juggernaut lives on, but as a whole, the move to Greek yogurt has allowed froyo to grow up. Like gelato, it is regarded as an interesting ice cream variant, not a dieter's substitute. You'll see that here, as the tart, rich frozen yogurt finds grounding with an earthy celery root mousse. Its texture does just the opposite—lightens it to a silky cloud. For this recipe, you will need a professional whip canister and two full chargers, available at gourmet stores or online.

SERVES 6

CELERY ROOT MOUSSE
2½ cups (700 grams) milk
1¼ cups (250 grams) heavy cream
1½ cups (300 grams) sugar
9 ounces (250 grams) celery root
Salt
5 sheets silver gelatin (see Note)
3½ tablespoons (50 grams) cold butter, cubed

FROZEN YOGURT
1 quart European-style yogurt
½ cup corn syrup
⅔ cup (133 grams) sugar

TO ASSEMBLE
3 whole passion fruits, halved

To make the celery root mousse: Using a chef's or paring knife, slice off the rooted area and bottom of the celery root. Roughly trim the sides and remove spots, as you would a potato, then peel. You will lose a large amount of volume. Soak in lemon-squeezed water if not using immediately, or coarsely grate the remaining celery root.

In a saucepan, combine the milk, cream, sugar, and celery root and bring to a boil over medium heat. Remove from the heat and allow the mixture to steep like a tea. After 30 to 45 minutes, the celery root will have infused the cream mixture with a subtle, not overpowering, flavor. Strain the infused liquid and discard the celery root. Season very lightly with salt, just to coax out the flavor of the celery root. Set aside.

Place the sheets of gelatin in a bowl of ice water. When soft and pliable, remove the sheets and squeeze out the excess water. Whisk the softened gelatin into the celery root liquid until fully dissolved. Whisk in the cold butter, piece by piece, until smooth. Refrigerate for 3 hours. Once the mousse has chilled, pour into a clean whip canister.

To make the frozen yogurt: Chill the bowl of an ice cream maker per the manufacturer's instructions—for frozen yogurt, the bowl needs to be as cold as possible.

In a medium bowl, stir together the yogurt, corn syrup, and sugar until just combined. Pour into the bowl of the ice cream maker; process according to the manufacturer's instructions.

CONTINUED

Frozen Yogurt with Whipped Celery Root Mousse and Passion Fruit

CONTINUED

Transfer the finished yogurt to a storage container and freeze until ready to serve.

To assemble: Place a large scoop of the finished frozen yogurt into individual bowls or plates.

Keeping the tip of the canister pointed straight down over, carefully dispense the mousse in cloud-like dollops over each scoop of yogurt (do not overshake the canister or shake between dispensing). Scoop out the passion fruit seeds and divide over each as topping. Serve immediately.

Note: Of sheet gelatin, silver is the most popular strength used in professional kitchens (bronze, gold, and platinum are also available). By strength, the idea is that platinum grade will produce a firmer end product than bronze. If only powdered gelatin is available, substitute 1.68 grams per 1 sheet of silver gelatin, or 8.4 grams. Gelatin, unless marked otherwise, is decidedly not vegan-friendly.

Proof Bakery / Flourless Chocolate Cake

In Atwater Village's lovely little Proof Bakery, Na Young Ma possesses a second sense for what to keep classic (a simple prune galette), and what to improvise with modern flavor (black sesame financier). Satisfying the former, here a versatile rich, flourless chocolate cake stuns in its purest form. It feels so essential, so straightforward and low-tech to master, so very much like a back-pocket recipe. Dense and moist, it's nut-free and sweetened with a little bit of sugar and honey. If you deliberately overbake it, the crust and sides crunch up enough to approximate a seriously chocolate-forward brownie.

MAKES ONE 8-INCH CAKE

12 ounces dark chocolate (70% cacao), chopped

½ cup (1 stick) butter

1 tablespoon honey

2 tablespoons unsweetened cocoa powder

¼ teaspoon table salt

4 egg yolks, room temperature

6 egg whites

½ cup plus 1 tablespoon (4 ounces) sugar

Cacao nibs, for garnish

Preheat the oven to 325°F. Lightly grease an 8-inch round cake pan or spray with nonstick cooking spray.

In the top of a double boiler (or in a heatproof bowl set over a pot of simmering water—be sure the water does not touch the the bottom of the bowl), whisk together the chocolate, butter, and honey until melted and well combined. Stir in the cocoa powder and salt. While the chocolate mixture is still warm—but barely—very slowly whisk in the egg yolks until fully incorporated.

Remove from the heat and allow to cool while you prepare the egg whites: In the bowl of a stand mixer fitted with the whisk attachment or using a hand mixer, beat the egg whites, very slowly adding the sugar until the mixture holds stiff peaks. Using a spatula and a large bowl, very gently fold the egg white mixture into the still-warm chocolate mixture in thirds—do not overdo it or you'll deflate the egg whites. (Worst case scenario: Your cake will be heavier.) You still want to see a few white ribbons running throughout. Pour the batter into the prepared pan. Sprinkle with cacao nibs.

Bake for 35 to 45 minutes, until a toothpick inserted into the center comes out clean. The cake should be just pulling away from the sides with a slight crust, fudgy, but fully cooked through (not molten in the middle like lava cake). Serve warm or at room temperature. Ice cream, whipped cream, and caramel sauce all gild the lily.

Spago Beverly Hills / Almond-Ginger Cake with Crème Fraîche Whipped Cream and Tangerine-Yuzu Reduction

This deconstructed vacherin shows how pastry chef Della Gossett has taken on the mantle of Spago's legendary desserts: an almond-ginger cake of buttery, superfine crumb served artfully with shards of crushed meringue; swooshes of whipped cream; quenelles of vanilla crème fraîche ice cream and tangerine sherbet; tangerine suprêmes (see Note); and a citrus reduction spooned around the plate. Edible nasturtium flowers garnish the dainty confection.

We've skipped straight to the cake in this streamlined adaptation of bright winter fruit, cake, and cream. Depending on your preference for individual or whole desserts, bake using a 13 by 18-inch rimmed baking sheet or a loaf pan; instructions for both are included. In lieu of homemade ice cream, a quality store-bought sherbet and vanilla ice cream will do nicely. Keep in mind when shopping that almond marzipan is the candy that molds into cool shapes and figures, while almond paste offers a coarser grind and less sweetness.

SERVES 6 TO 8

ALMOND-GINGER CAKE
Generous ¾ cup (75 grams) cake flour

1 teaspoon (4 grams) baking powder

Pinch of salt

Generous ¾ cup (151 grams) almond paste

Generous ½ cup (116 grams) sugar

⅔ cup (1⅓ sticks / 151 grams) butter

4 eggs

½ teaspoon (2⅓ grams) vanilla extract

2 teaspoons (9½ grams) grated fresh ginger

TANGERINE-YUZU REDUCTION
1 pint tangerine juice

1¼ tablespoons (15 grams) sugar

Yuzu juice

CRÈME FRAÎCHE WHIPPED CREAM
1 cup (226 grams) heavy cream

½ cup (113 grams) crème fraîche

4 teaspoons (14 grams) sugar

To make the almond-ginger cake: Preheat the oven to 350°F.

In a medium bowl, sift together the cake flour, baking powder, and salt.

In a food processor, pulverize the almond paste and sugar until fine and crumbly. With the machine running, add in the butter and process to a smooth paste. Transfer to the bowl of a stand mixer fitted with the paddle attachment. On medium speed, add the eggs 2 at a time, beating well for 2 minutes after each addition and stopping to scrape down the bowl between additions. When fully combined, add the vanilla and ginger. Reduce the speed to low, then gradually mix in the dry ingredients until the batter is uniform.

Line a 13 by 18-inch rimmed baking sheet or loaf pan with parchment paper. Grease or spray the pan and pour in the batter. Tap the pan against the counter to release any air bubbles, and spread it evenly. Bake until the cake is a strong golden brown, the top springs back when pressed, and a toothpick inserted into the center comes out clean, about 25 minutes for the baking sheet or 35 minutes for the loaf pan. (If it's browning too quickly, tent it with foil about halfway through.)

Let cool in the pan on a wire rack for 15 to 20 minutes. The cake will deflate a bit. Remove from the loaf pan and slice, or if you're individually plating, cut out 3-inch circles with a round cookie cutter.

CONTINUED

TO ASSEMBLE

1 satsuma tangerine, cut into suprêmes (see Note)

Vanilla ice cream (optional)

Tangerine sherbet (optional)

Edible flowers (optional)

Crumbled meringues (optional)

To make the tangerine-yuzu reduction: In a small saucepan, bring the tangerine juice and sugar to a boil. Cook until slightly thickened. Remove from the heat and let cool, then add yuzu juice according to taste, a tiny splash at a time. Set aside.

To make the crème fraîche whipped cream: In a large bowl or in the bowl of a stand mixer fitted with the whisk attachment, whisk all the whipped cream ingredients on medium-high speed until the cream holds soft peaks. Cover tightly and refrigerate until ready to use.

To assemble: On a plate, arrange slices or rounds of cake and top each with a dollop of crème fraîche whipped cream, tangerine segments, a drizzle of tangerine-yuzu reduction, and a garnish of edible flowers, if you wish. Serve with vanilla ice cream and sherbet alongside, and crushed meringues, if you wish. Store leftover cake in the freezer, wrapped in foil and sealed in an airtight container.

Note: Peeling the membrane and pith of a fruit isn't done in vain; it removes any potential bitterness. There's a high gastronomy cheat for perfect suprêmes called Pectinex Ultra SP-L (available online). Soaking fruit segments in water and Pectinex Ultra SP-L breaks down the structure of the membranes so they slip off. If that's not your style, you can go the old-fashioned route: Slice the bottom off the fruit just so it sits flat on your cutting board. Cut down around the outside curve of the fruit, removing the peel and white pith. Holding the fruit over a bowl, cut alongside the membranes between the segments of fruit and allow the segments to fall into the bowl.

Little Flower Candy Co. / Olive Oil Cake with Brown Butter Frosting

While money doesn't grow on trees in Los Angeles, winter citrus does! During this bountiful season, heavy, crinkled paper bags of fruit emblazoned with "Take Me" signs begin to appear in office kitchens, schools, yoga studios, and day cares. Sunday projects like marmalade, limoncello, and olive oil cake are generally the result. Given this annual ritual, a cake considered traditionally Italian feels quite Californian to me.

Room-temperature ingredients, especially the eggs, are clutch in this recipe—one even a novice baker can slay. To balance the fruity olive oil and citrus flavors, Cecilia Leung and Christine Moore of Little Flower Candy Co. add a whipped frosting with a nutty brown-butter base. To serve with candied kumquats, as they do, check out the recipe from Daughter's Granola, on page 204. Another reason to love olive oil cake: Many desserts grow stale by the hour, yet this one improves in flavor and texture after a day or two.

MAKES ONE 9-INCH CAKE

OLIVE OIL CAKE

2 cups (240 grams) all-purpose flour

1¾ cups (350 grams) sugar

1½ teaspoons sea salt

½ teaspoon baking soda

½ teaspoon baking powder

3 eggs, at room temperature

1¼ cups (250 grams) extra-virgin olive oil

1¼ cups (250 grams) milk

1 tablespoon orange zest

½ cup (110 grams) fresh orange juice

BROWN BUTTER FROSTING

½ cup brown butter (see page 204), at room temperature

1½ cups plus 3 tablespoons (192 grams) powdered sugar

½ teaspoon sea salt

¾ teaspoon pure vanilla extract

1 teaspoon heavy cream

1 teaspoon milk

Fresh berries or edible flowers, for garnish, optional

To make the olive oil cake: Preheat the oven to 375°F. Line a 9-inch round cake pan with parchment paper cut to fit. Lightly coat the parchment with nonstick spray on both sides.

Into a medium bowl, sift together the flour, sugar, salt, baking soda, and baking powder.

In the bowl of a stand mixer fitted with the whisk attachment, beat the eggs on medium speed, until the texture becomes thicker, yet lighter, and the color begins to pale, about 2 minutes.

With the machine running on medium speed, stream in the olive oil as slowly as you can, stopping to scrape down the sides of the bowl if necessary. Mix until the mixture thickens slightly and begins to become opaque, 2 to 3 minutes. Lower the speed one notch. Carefully stream in the milk, then add the orange zest and juice and mix until just combined.

Lower the mixer speed again. Working ½ cup at a time so as to avoid a pouf of flour in your face, add the dry ingredients. Mix only until fully incorporated, about 30 seconds. Stop the mixer and using a rubber spatula, scrape the bowl to ensure no pockets of dry ingredients remain. The consistency should resemble pancake batter.

Pour the batter into the prepared pan. Bake until the cake begins to dome, about 30 minutes, then rotate the pan and bake for 30 minutes more. The cake will be ready when the top turns a dark golden brown and just begins to split, the sides pull away, and a toothpick inserted into the center of the cake comes out clean.

CONTINUED

Olive Oil Cake with Brown Butter Frosting
CONTINUED

Meanwhile, make the frosting: In the bowl of a stand mixer fitted with the paddle attachment, cream the brown butter on medium speed until lightened in color and fluffy, about 2 minutes.

Reduce the speed to low. Slowly add the powdered sugar in ½-cup increments, stopping to scrape down the bowl after each addition. When the buttercream begins to appear light and fluffy, stop the mixer and scrape down the sides again.

With the mixer running, add the salt and vanilla. Stop the mixer and scrape the bowl. Restart the mixer and pour in the cream and milk. Increase the speed to medium and mix until incorporated. Stop the mixer and scrape the bowl. Increase the speed to medium-high. Cream the frosting until light, shiny, and fluffy, about 2 minutes. (Do not overbeat or mix on a high speed, or the buttercream will begin to separate and melt.)

Use immediately, or transfer the buttercream to an airtight container and refrigerate for up to 2 weeks. If refrigerating, let the frosting come to room temperature so it's spreadable before use.

Allow the cake to cool in the pan for at least 2 hours, then turn the cake out onto a serving pedestal or platter. Using an offset spatula or wooden spoon, cover the top of the cake with the brown butter frosting, and, if desired, decorate the cake with fresh berries or edible flowers.

Jon & Vinny's / Rosemary–Pine Nut Tart

Here, a so-very-Italian flavor combination of rosemary and pine nuts sprinkled about a layer of pastry cream and brown butter filling tops a shortbread-like *pâte sucrée* shell. The taste of Tuscany gone California is a worthy way to seal off pizza night at the neighborhood joint that everyone wishes was a stroll down the street. It is kissed with a dollop of soft whipped crème fraîche (page 218) and sea salt caramel.

Remember to refrigerate the crust after you roll it out. If you're making the sweet crust in advance, cover the shell in two layers of plastic wrap, then foil, and refrigerate for up to 2 days or freeze up to 1 week before baking. Any leftover or scraps of dough also make an amazing shortbread, which can be fashioned into delicious button-sized cookies (see page 237).

MAKES ONE 9-INCH TART OR EIGHT 4-INCH TARTS

PASTRY CREAM
4 cups milk

1 cup plus 2 tablespoons sugar

½ vanilla bean

¼ teaspoon salt

½ cup (2¼ ounces) cornstarch

2 egg yolks, at room temperature

3 eggs

6 tablespoons (¾ stick / 171 grams) cold butter, cubed

PÂTE SUCRÉE
3¾ cups (16 ounces) all-purpose flour, plus more for dusting

1 cup plus 2 tablespoons (8 ounces) sugar

1¼ teaspoons (¼ ounce) salt

1 cup (2 sticks / 227 grams) cold butter, cubed

1 egg

2 egg yolks

1 tablespoon heavy cream

BROWN BUTTER FILLING
1¼ cups (2½ sticks / 341 grams) butter

1 vanilla bean, seeds scraped from the pod

To make the pastry cream: In a large stockpot, combine the milk, 1 cup plus 1 tablespoon of the sugar, the vanilla, and salt. Heat the mixture over medium-low heat. Do not bring the mixture to a boil; instead, look for the moment just before, when small bubbles begin to form on the edges, a barely visible skin forms on the surface, and the milk begins to steam. As soon as you reach this point, remove from the heat and let cool for 5 minutes.

In a bowl, whisk together the cornstarch and remaining 1 tablespoon sugar. Slowly whisk in the egg yolks and eggs. To temper the milk, add a ladleful of milk to the egg mixture; whisk well to combine. Add another ladleful and whisk again; repeat with a third ladleful. While whisking continuously, very slowly pour the egg-milk mixture into the pot with the remaining milk mixture and return the pot to low heat until the cream thickens noticeably.

Transfer the pastry cream to a food processor. With the machine running, gradually add the cubed butter until the mixture has a smooth consistency. Let cool; when the cream has almost cooled to room temperature, transfer to an airtight container and press plastic wrap directly against the surface to prevent a skin from forming. Refrigerate for at least 8 hours and up to 3 days.

To prepare the pâte sucrée: In the bowl of a stand mixer fitted with the paddle attachment, mix together the flour, sugar, and salt. With the machine running on medium speed, add the butter and mix until the butter resembles pebbles. Add the egg and egg yolks, one at a time, and mix until emulsified. Add the cream and mix until the dough just comes together. Turn out onto a lightly floured surface and knead until just smooth. Wrap the ball of dough tightly in plastic wrap and chill.

CONTINUED

Rosemary–Pine Nut Tart

CONTINUED

Generous 1¾ cups (13⅓ ounces) sugar

¾ cup plus ⅛ cup (3 ounces) cake flour

5 eggs

TO ASSEMBLE

1 cup raw pine nuts

Leaves from 2 rosemary sprigs, finely chopped

Crème Fraîche Whipped Cream (page 218)

Fleur de sel

Caramel Sauce (page 235)

To make the brown butter filling: In a saucepan, combine the butter and vanilla bean pod and seeds. Cook over medium heat until fragrant, nutty, and browned, swirling the pan as the butter begins to foam up. It will pass from bright yellow to gold to a kraft-paper brown to a lager brown and browned bits will form on the bottom, about 9 minutes. The smell should be nutty. Remove from the heat and let the brown butter cool, then remove and discard the vanilla bean pod.

In the bowl of a stand mixer fitted with the whisk attachment, beat together the sugar and flour on medium-high speed. Add the eggs, waiting until each is incorporated before adding the next. Beat until the batter is light and fluffy. Gradually add the brown butter and mix to combine. Set aside.

To bake the tart: Preheat the oven to 350°F.

Remove the dough from the fridge and let it come almost to room temperature. On a lightly floured surface, roll out the dough to ⅛ inch thick. Line one 9-inch tart pan or 8 individual 4-inch pans with the dough and refrigerate.

Spread a thin (¼-inch-thick) layer of pastry cream over the dough. Sprinkle a generous amount of pine nuts on top of the pastry cream, and repeat with the rosemary. Pour in the brown butter filling to a depth of ⅛ inch from the top of the tart pan. Sprinkle again with the remaining rosemary and pine nuts.

Bake immediately, rotating the tart(s) halfway through, until the filling is golden brown across the top and the center no longer jiggles, about 25 minutes for 4-inch tarts and a bit longer for a 9-inch tart. Serve warm with crème fraîche whipped cream and fleur de sel–sprinkled caramel sauce.

Rucker's Pies / Berry Lattice Pie

The keys to the piecrust castle are lard, lard, and lard. Though Nicole Rucker has been baking for most of her life, she really found her calling as pastry chef for the Gjelina group, especially opening Gjelina Take Away, when they developed a loyal following for their sourdoughs and sweets. Rucker won the blue ribbon at the APC National Pie Championship in Orlando the first year she entered, and subsequently nabbed four out of seven possible blue ribbons available at the KCRW Good Food Pie Contest—in a single year. She popped up everywhere, making pastries for Cofax (see page 18), delivering hand pies to Dinosaur Coffee and Bludso's, and, eventually, she launched Rucker's Pies. Instead of hoarding those recipes, she's as generous as can be.

SERVES 4 TO 6

PIE DOUGH
3½ ounces hot water
1 tablespoon brown sugar
1 teaspoon apple cider vinegar
7 ounces (scant 1 cup / 1¾ sticks) butter, cold
3 ounces lard (or butter)
3 cups all-purpose flour
1 teaspoon fine sea salt

BERRY-RHUBARB FILLING
8 ounces rhubarb, cut into ½-inch pieces
12 ounces raspberries
8 ounces strawberries, hulled and coarsely chopped
1½ cups granulated sugar
1½ ounces cornstarch
2 teaspoons ground cinnamon
Fresh lemon juice

TO ASSEMBLE
3 tablespoons heavy cream
3 tablespoons coarse sanding sugar

To make the dough: In a bowl, combine the hot water, brown sugar, and vinegar and stir until the sugar has dissolved. Refrigerate until very cold.

In a food processor, pulse the cold butter, lard, flour, and salt until the butter is the size of medium peas.

Turn the butter-flour mixture out onto a table and smear away from you, using the palm of your hand. Repeat until the butter is incorporated and the dough looks shaggy. Form into a hill, and make a well in the center. Pour half the chilled liquid into the center. Using your hands, mix from the center, incorporating the liquid into the dough slowly. Start to push and press the dough together to form a mass, sprinkling the remaining liquid on the shaggy mass until it comes together. Have patience with this.

Using a bench knife or pastry scraper, divide the dough into two discs. Wrap each in plastic, and chill at least 2 hours before using.

To prepare the filling: In a bowl, combine the filling ingredients. Set aside to macerate for 10 minutes, then adjust with the lemon juice.

When the dough is chilled, preheat the oven to 350°F.

To assemble: Set out the two dough discs on a well-floured surface. Before you roll out the pie dough, smack it with your rolling pin a few times. Working efficiently so the dough doesn't warm, roll out each disc into a 12-inch-thick round. Press one gently into a greased pie plate and trim the edges so there is a ½-inch overhang all around. Use a knife to trim long, even strips from the second round of dough.

Pour the filling into the prepared bottom crust. Arrange the strips over the top in a lattice pattern, folding the strips under the overhanging dough from the bottom crust and pinching or crimping with a fork to seal. Brush the strips with the cream and sprinkle with the coarse sugar. Bake for 1 hour, or until the crust darkens to golden brown and the juices boil up around the lattice. Transfer to a wire rack and cool for at least 2 hours before slicing and serving.

Pizzeria Mozza / Meyer Lemon Gelato Pie with Champagne Vinegar Sauce and Candied Lemon Zest

Thin-skinned as an insecure teenager, Meyer lemons are unusually sweet, orange-kissed, and less acidic than their puckery, sunny friends. They're quite common in California but an impressive specialty in other areas. In season, you'll see them flavoring gelato; candied for olive oil cakes; and juiced and zested for lemon bars. They also dance all over savory preparations, charred, preserved, and packed in salt for salads and vinaigrettes.

In this nod to the no-bake ice cream pie and lemon meringue pie, L.A. culinary icon Nancy Silverton gives us dreamy Meyer lemon gelato packed into a graham cracker crust, dolloped with whipped cream. (Their graham crackers are homemade!) The sweet-acid one-two punch of a champagne vinegar caramel sauce and candied lemon peel caps off this cool slice of heaven. Good quality lemon gelato, or any flavor you like, works if you don't have an ice cream maker.

SERVES 6 TO 8

MEYER LEMON GELATO
3 tablespoons cornstarch
4 cups milk
½ cup plus 2 tablespoons sugar
¼ cup nonfat dry milk powder
¼ cup light corn syrup
⅛ teaspoon Diamond Crystal kosher salt
Zest of 2 Meyer lemons
1¼ cups strained fresh Meyer lemon juice (from 5 to 8 Meyer lemons)
½ cup heavy cream

GRAHAM CRACKER CRUST
1 cup graham cracker crumbs
1 cup (2 sticks) butter, melted
1 cup sugar
¼ teaspoon ground cinnamon

CANDIED LEMON ZEST
2 lemons
1¾ cups sugar
2 tablespoons light corn syrup

To make the Meyer lemon gelato: Fill a large bowl with ice and water and set a smaller bowl inside. Set a fine-mesh strainer in the smaller bowl. In a medium bowl, whisk the cornstarch and 1 cup of the milk together until the cornstarch has dissolved.

In a 4-quart saucepan, combine ½ cup of the sugar, the milk powder, corn syrup, salt, and the remaining 3 cups milk. Heat over high heat, using a whisk to break up and dissolve the milk powder, until the mixture just begins to bubble.

Remove from the heat and while whisking continuously, gradually add the milk-cornstarch slurry. Return the saucepan to high heat. Bring to a boil, then reduce the heat to medium-high. Cook, whisking continuously, until the gelato base thickens slightly, 4 to 5 minutes. The gelato base should become viscous but it will not thicken enough to coat the back of a spoon.

Strain the gelato base into the smaller bowl in the ice bath to cool. Once it reaches room temperature, set aside. Transfer to an airtight container, and refrigerate for several hours and up to 3 days.

Pour the chilled gelato base into a large bowl. In a small bowl, stir together the Meyer lemon zest, Meyer lemon juice, and remaining 2 tablespoons sugar until the sugar has dissolved. Add the lemon mixture and the heavy cream to the gelato base and whisk to combine. Pour the Meyer lemon gelato base into an ice cream maker and churn according to the manufacturer's instructions. Transfer the finished gelato to a storage container and freeze until you're ready to fill the pie. (The texture will be most giving for filling the pie within a few hours of spinning.)

CONTINUED

Meyer Lemon Gelato Pie with Champagne Vinegar Sauce and Candied Lemon Zest

CONTINUED

CHAMPAGNE VINEGAR SAUCE

2 cups sugar (only granulated sugar will work)

½ cup water

1 vanilla bean

½ cup champagne vinegar

2 tablespoons butter, cubed

WHIPPED CREAM

1 cup very cold heavy cream

5 tablespoons crème fraîche or sour cream

To make the graham cracker crust: Preheat the oven to 350°F. Grease a 9-inch glass or aluminum pie plate.

In a bowl, stir together the graham cracker crumbs, melted butter, sugar, and cinnamon. Press the crumbs into the bottom and sides of the prepared pie plate to form an even crust. Place the crust on a baking sheet and bake until firm, about 8 minutes. Transfer to a rack to cool. Once the crust has reached room temperature, cover and place in the freezer. (The crust will keep in the freezer for up to a week.)

Spoon the gelato into the prepared pie shell. Using an offset or rubber spatula, create a wavy surface. Cover with plastic wrap and place the pie in the freezer for several hours or overnight, to freeze completely.

While the pie is in the freezer, make the candied lemon zest: Using a vegetable peeler, pull long, irregular strips of peel from the lemons. (Reserve the lemons for another use.) Place the peel in a small, heavy-bottomed saucepan and cover with water. Bring the water to a boil over high heat. Remove from the heat, use a fine-mesh strainer to remove the peel, and drain the water. Return the peel to the saucepan and cover again with water. Bring to a boil, then turn off the heat, strain, and drain. Repeat this process a third time, then set the lemon peel aside.

Clean and dry the saucepan and set it over high heat. Add the sugar, corn syrup, and 2 cups water. Bring to a boil. Dip a pastry brush in water and brush down the sides of the pot to remove any sugar crystals. Once the mixture boils, add the lemon peel, reduce the heat, and simmer, brushing down the sides occasionally, until the peel is tender, translucent, and candied, about 20 minutes. Remove from the heat and set aside to cool to room temperature. If not using immediately, transfer the strips to an airtight container and store them at room temperature for up to several weeks.

To make the champagne vinegar sauce: Fill a large bowl with ice and water. Set a smaller bowl inside. Fit a fine-mesh strainer in the smaller bowl. In a large, heavy-bottomed saucepan, combine the sugar and water. Bring to a boil over high heat without stirring. As sugar crystals form on the sides of the pan, dip a pastry brush in water and brush down. Using a small, sharp knife, split the vanilla bean lengthwise, and use the back of the knife to scrape the pulp and seeds into the saucepan. Add the pod as well.

Cook the sugar, without stirring. You want the sugar to cook evenly without brown or hot spots, so swirl the pan and occasionally brush down the sides of the pan. When the sugar begins to show color around the edges, 4 to 5 minutes, use a wooden spoon to begin stirring the mixture gently. Cook and gently stir until the caramel is translucent and medium amber-colored. (If it becomes cloudy or grainy, stir and swirl the pan until the sugar melts.)

Remove from the heat and stir in the vinegar. (Be mindful, as the hot mixture will spatter.) The sauce may seize and harden, which is normal—return the saucepan to medium-high heat and boil until the sauce melts (if it has seized), about 3 minutes. Once the sauce begins to reduce and thicken slightly, about 5 minutes, turn off the heat. Whisk in the butter gently, a few pieces at a time as the sauce foams, until fully emulsified. The sauce should be tart-sweet, and slightly sticky to the touch. If too runny, continue to reduce over medium heat for 1 to 2 minutes more, and test again.

Strain the sauce into the smaller bowl set in the ice bath. Remove and discard the vanilla bean pod. Allow the sauce to cool in the bath to a syrupy consistency, whisking occasionally to prevent the butter from separating. If not using immediately, transfer to an airtight container and refrigerate for up to several weeks. (Reheat the sauce over low heat and let cool until syrupy.)

To make the whipped cream: Chill a large metal bowl and whisk until very cold. Pour the heavy cream into the chilled bowl and whisk until it thickens to soft peaks. (Don't overwhip or the cream will curdle.) Add the crème fraîche and gently beat to a thick, mousse-like consistency. Cover the bowl and refrigerate until ready to use. If the cream has separated, whip gently to re-stiffen before serving.

To assemble: Using a large knife, cut the pie into 6 or 8 equal wedges; dipping the knife into hot water and wiping it dry between cuts. Spoon 1 tablespoon of the champagne vinegar sauce on each plate and, using the back of the spoon, spread it into a circle. Top with a slice of pie. Garnish each slice with 2 generous tablespoons of whipped cream, an additional tablespoon of the champagne sauce, and 3 strips of candied lemon peel.

Valerie Confections / "Fallen Fruit" Cake

When it comes to showpiece cakes in Los Angeles, Valerie Gordon tops the short list. At first, she was connecting with the spirit of famed L.A. landmarks such as the Scandia apple cake and the Brown Derby grapefruit cake. Now, tomorrow's classics is her thing. This gorgeous layer cake is her elegant offering for your next special occasion: "Fallen Fruit," a moist vanilla cake cushioned with petal-pink raspberry buttercream and ripe berries and figs, all covered with more fresh buttercream (this time, lemon!) and even more fruit.

For the most even results, bake the layers individually. You can prep and refrigerate the buttercream up to a week ahead of time. Don't worry if it becomes hard as a rock. When you're ready to finish the cake, allow the chilled buttercream to rest at room temperature for a half hour, then place it into the bowl of a stand mixer fitted with the paddle attachment and beat until light and fluffy. For three layers (or more), make an additional half-portion of the batter for each tier added and double the buttercream in order to completely enrobe the finished cake. Tailor the "fallen" fruit to your preference or the season.

SERVES 8 TO 10

VANILLA CAKE

3¼ cups (16¼ ounces) cake flour

¾ teaspoon (5¼ grams) baking powder

1 teaspoon (3 grams) Diamond Crystal kosher salt

1½ cups plus 6 tablespoons (3¾ sticks) butter

2 tablespoons corn syrup

2 cups (14 ounces) granulated sugar

6 eggs

¼ cup (2 ounces) crème fraîche or sour cream

2 tablespoons vanilla paste

LEMON AND RASPBERRY BUTTERCREAM

3 cups (6 sticks / 24 ounces) butter

1½ cups (6¾ ounces) powdered sugar

¼ cup plus 2 tablespoons (3 ounces) light corn syrup

1 tablespoon pure vanilla extract

2 tablespoons lemon juice

Pinch of salt

12 ounces white chocolate, melted and cooled

⅔ cup (6 ounces) raspberry jam

To make the vanilla cake: Preheat the oven to 350°F. Trace and cut out circles of parchment to fit two 9 by 3-inch round cake pans. Coat the bottom and sides with nonstick spray or butter, then line with the parchment.

Into a medium bowl, sift together the flour, baking powder, and salt. In the bowl of a stand mixer fitted with the paddle attachment, cream the butter, corn syrup, and granulated sugar on medium speed until light and fluffy. Stop and scrape down the sides of the bowl.

Meanwhile, in a small bowl, whisk the eggs, crème fraîche, and vanilla paste until well incorporated. With the mixer running on medium speed, pour the egg mixture into the creamed butter and beat until smooth.

Working in ½-cup increments, add the dry ingredients, mixing for about 30 seconds after each addition. Beat the batter until fully incorporated and smooth, stopping to scrape down the bowl as necessary.

Divide the batter equally between the cake pans and smooth the tops. Put one cake in the oven and bake for 20 minutes, then rotate and bake for 20 to 25 minutes more, until firm to the touch, matte in finish, the sides begin to pull away from the pan, and a toothpick inserted into the center comes out clean. Remove from the oven and let cool completely. Repeat with the second cake.

CONTINUED

"Fallen Fruit" Cake

CONTINUED

TO ASSEMBLE

3½ cups assorted berries, stemmed

1 pint small plums

1 pint assorted figs, grapes, and currants

1 pint kumquats, mandarinquats, or small seasonal citrus fruits

Meanwhile, to make the lemon and raspberry buttercream: In the bowl of a stand mixer fitted with the paddle attachment, beat the butter on medium to medium-high speed until very soft and creamy. Stop and scrape down the sides and bottom of the bowl, then beat for 1 minute more. In small increments, add the powdered sugar and look for a very light consistency before streaming in the corn syrup, vanilla, and lemon juice. Beat for 2 minutes more. Reduce the speed to low. Slowly pour in the melted white chocolate. Add the pinch of salt and stir until the buttercream is fluffy and shiny. Transfer to a separate bowl. Return 2 cups of the buttercream to the stand mixer bowl; cover and refrigerate the remainder.

With the mixer running on medium speed, beat the 2 cups buttercream with the jam until uniformly pink (no white streaks), about 2 minutes.

To assemble: Remove the cooled cakes from the pans. Place one cake upside-down on a turntable, if you have one. Evenly spread with 1 cup of the raspberry buttercream. Cover the buttercream with 1½ cups berries, then top with the remaining raspberry buttercream. Set the second cake, right side up, directly on top of the buttercream-and-berries layer. Press gently to adhere.

Using a large offset spatula, coat the entire cake with a thin layer of the reserved lemon buttercream, and chill to stiffen slightly, 30 minutes (this is your crumb coat). Using the back of a wooden spoon, thickly frost the top and sides of the cake with additional lemon buttercream, finishing with bold strokes.

To serve: Place the cake on a cake stand or dessert tray. Arrange the heavier fruit, such as plums, figs, or grapes in the center of the cake and around the base. By the handful, gently drop lighter fruits, such as currants, berries, and small citrus, over the cake so they mound on top and tumble down the sides.

Bottega Louie / Butterscotch Budino with Caramel Sauce

We wouldn't dare write a book about L.A. food without including the city's unofficial dessert. Be it Bottega Louie's, Mozza's, Jar's, or Gjelina's—the budino is a local modern icon. Well suited for advance preparation, this parfait-style layering of pudding and caramel is an all-around winner for any holiday. Think of caramel and butterscotch as first cousins separated only by molasses. The former takes white sugar; the latter, brown. Cream, butter, and vanilla unite them. If you can't find sheet gelatin, see page 216 for easy conversions.

Finish with a flourish: a sprinkle of fleur de sel, a dollop of crème fraîche whipped cream, and anything from rosemary shortbreads to smoked sea salt cookies to French macarons. At Bottega Louie, amid the echo of grand, tall bank columns, it's worth the wait for Neapolitan-style pizza and one of these desserts, and just try to resist leaving without a rainbow assortment of picture-perfect macarons.

MAKES TWELVE ½-CUP SERVINGS

CARAMEL SAUCE
2½ cups (500 grams) granulated sugar

⅓ cup (100 grams) light corn syrup

150 grams water

½ cup plus 6 tablespoons (1¾ sticks / 7 ounces) butter

2⅛ cups (16¾ ounces) heavy cream, warmed

1 teaspoon (5 grams) salt

BUDINO
2½ tablespoons (25 grams) cornstarch

2 eggs, at room temperature

3 egg yolks, at room temperature

1⅓ cups (228 grams) lightly packed muscovado or dark brown sugar

Scant ½ teaspoon (3 grams) salt

½ cup (118 grams) water

2¾ cups (683 grams) heavy cream

Scant 1½ cups (350 grams) milk

2 silver gelatin sheets, bloomed in cold water for 5 to 10 minutes and squeezed dry (or 1⅛ teaspoons powdered gelatin)

4 tablespoons (½ stick / 56 grams) butter, cubed, room temperature

To make the caramel sauce: Fill a large bowl with ice and water. Set a smaller bowl inside. Fit a fine-mesh strainer in the smaller bowl.

In a medium pot, combine the granulated sugar, corn syrup, and water over low heat. Stir once with a wooden spoon or spatula, then leave alone as the water evaporates and boils. As sugar crystals form on the sides, dip a pastry brush in water and brush down the sides of the pan. Continue to cook the sugar, without stirring, 4 to 5 minutes. You want the sugar to cook evenly without brown or hot spots, so swirl the pan and occasionally brush down the sides of the pan.

When the sugar does begin to show color around the edges, stir slowly with the wooden spoon. You will be watching as the color quickly changes from lemon yellow to amber to mahogany and dark brown. Especially if you're not using a candy thermometer, better to be conservative as you judge the color. Cook and gently stir until the caramel is translucent and medium amber-colored. (If it becomes cloudy or grainy, continue to stir and swirl the pan until the sugar melts.) You are looking to reach a medium amber color, or if using a candy thermometer, caramelizing around 360°F. The longer it cooks, the more bitter and complex the flavor will get. Especially if you're not using a candy thermometer, better to be conservative as you judge the color.

The moment you hit your color, remove from the heat and very quickly add the butter and warm cream. Be mindful, as the hot mixture will roil, but keep stirring carefully. Return the pot to medium-high heat. Whisk or stir continuously as the mixture

CONTINUED

Butterscotch Budino with Caramel Sauce
CONTINUED

begins to reduce and thicken into an emulsified sauce, about 2 minutes. It should be barely sticky to the touch and pliable, not runny. If too runny, cook over medium heat for an additional minute and test again.

Remove from the heat, add the salt, and pass through the prepared strainer into the bowl set in the ice bath. Cover and refrigerate.

To make the budino: In a bowl with a spout, make a slurry by whisking together the cornstarch, eggs, and egg yolks. Set aside.

In a large saucepan, combine the muscovado sugar, salt, and water and stir. Bring to a boil over medium-low heat and allow the mixture to reach 220°F on a candy thermometer.

Remove from the heat and quickly add the cream and milk, stirring continuously. Return the pot to a boil over medium-high heat. (It'll foam up like mad, so a large pot will keep you from spending an hour cleaning your stove.)

Add a ladleful of the hot sugar-milk-cream mixture to the egg mixture; whisk well. Repeat twice more to temper the eggs.

Off the heat, very slowly pour the egg mixture into the pot, whisking well to combine. Return the pot to a boil to activate the cornstarch, stirring briskly to avoid burning. As it thickens, keep stirring until it reaches the thickness of shaving cream, about 5 minutes.

Remove from the heat and add the gelatin, then the butter, and stir until incorporated.

Strain the budino batter through a chinois into a container. Cover with plastic wrap pressed directly against the surface to prevent a skin from forming. Allow it to cool slightly, but you want it warm before layering each portion. You should have just shy of 6 cups of budino.

To assemble: Set out 12 small glass tumblers, ramekins, or cups on a tray. First, add a bottom layer of ¼ cup (60 grams) of the budino batter and freeze the tray for a few minutes, until the budino sets. Next, add the layer of 2 tablespoons (30 grams) of the caramel and freeze until set. Add another layer of the budino on top, and another layer of caramel, if you wish.

To serve: Wrap tightly and freeze. Before serving, make sure to leave the budinos out for a good hour or the caramel will be hard as a rock. Finish with a dollop of crème fraîche whipped cream (see page 218) and savory or sweet cookies for crunch.

Church & State / Pots de Crème au Chocolat

Of this silky textured French classic by the great Tony Esnault, my editor says, "I wouldn't kick a pot de crème out of bed." [Editor's note: This is 100% true.] This espresso-spiked moment of deep chocolate will remind you of the difficulty in deposing chocolate as king of desserts. It's a dinner party recipe that you can make far ahead. Serve these individual sweets with fresh whipped crème fraîche, cocoa powder, fleur de sel, or chocolate shavings. Crunchy cookies like tuiles and biscotti make a fine accompaniment, too.

Yes, you can freeze leftover cartons of cream. When you're ready, thaw in the refrigerator for a day or so, and shake exceptionally well to redistribute the butterfat, especially if it has lost its emulsion.

MAKES TWELVE ½-CUP SERVINGS

4 cups heavy cream
1 shot decaffeinated espresso
⅔ cups (125 grams) sugar
8 egg yolks
6 ounces / 170 grams dark chocolate (64% cacao), grated (about 1¼ cups)

Preheat the oven to 350°F. Set twelve 2¾-inch small ramekins or six 3½-inch ramekins in a rimmed baking pan. Bring a kettle or pot of water to boil.

In a saucepan, combine the cream, espresso, and sugar. Clip a candy thermometer to the side and heat the mixture over medium-low heat until it reaches 180°F, stirring with a wooden spoon to dissolve the sugar, about 12 minutes.

In a separate bowl, whisk the egg yolks. Add a ladleful of the hot cream mixture to the eggs and whisk well to combine. Add another ladleful and whisk again to temper the eggs. Gradually pour the egg mixture over the grated chocolate, and whisk to incorporate. Pour this mixture back into the saucepan and return to the stove, stirring continuously over the heat as the mixture thickens, about 6 minutes. Once well incorporated, remove from the heat.

Divide the mixture evenly among the ramekins.

Gently pour enough hot water into the baking pan to come about 1 inch up the sides of the ramekins. Cover the pan with foil, and transfer to the oven. Bake for 30 to 33 minutes, until the custard is barely set and still a tad jiggly when shaken (it'll continue to firm as it cools).

Carefully remove the ramekins from the hot water and transfer to a wire rack to cool. Cover each ramekin, and refrigerate until chilled. (Finished pots de crème will keep, wrapped tightly with plastic wrap directly against the surface of the custard, for up to 3 days.)

The Sycamore Kitchen / Salted Chocolate Chip Rye Cookies

Of course there's a chocolate chip cookie—I wouldn't leave you hanging.

Thank the eastern Europeans for their chocolate-rye breads, and Danes for topping their breakfast *rugbrød*—a dark and dense, seedy rye pressed together as if with hydraulic force—with slivers of fine dark chocolate (*Pålægschokolade*). We have Karen Hatfield of Sycamore Kitchen to thank for these salty-sweet numbers infused with caraway.

In the world of cookie tinkering, the molasses content in dark sugar lends chewiness, while white sugar is responsible for snap and crunch: Adjust depending on your tastes. When making the dough, rye flour gets sticky, so chilling keeps the dough from spreading when baked. Folks wildly insistent on a chewy-cakey texture can add an additional egg yolk. Semisweet chips make for a slightly less sophisticated, if crowd-pleasing, cookie.

MAKES 18 COOKIES

¾ cup (1½ sticks / 6 ounces) butter, at room temperature, cubed

¾ cup (5 ounces) loosely packed dark brown sugar

Generous ½ cup (4 ounces) granulated sugar

1 egg

2 teaspoons pure vanilla extract

1 cup (4¼ ounces) all-purpose flour

1 cup (3¾ ounces) rye flour

¼ teaspoon plus ⅛ teaspoon baking soda

¾ teaspoon baking powder

¾ teaspoon (2¼ grams) Diamond Crystal kosher salt

¼ teaspoon plus ⅛ teaspoon ground caraway seed

1 cup (6 ounces) dark chocolate (70% cacao), chopped

Fleur de sel, for sprinkling

To make the dough: In the bowl of a stand mixer fitted with the paddle attachment, cream the butter and both sugars together on low speed for 10 minutes. Add the egg and vanilla and mix for 1 minute, or until combined. Add the dry ingredients. Mix until almost incorporated, scraping down the bowl as necessary. Add the chocolate and give it one last quick mix. Wrap the dough in plastic and chill for about 1 hour or up to 3 days.

Preheat the oven to 350°F. Line a rimmed baking sheet with parchment paper or a silicone baking mat.

Remove the dough from the refrigerator and let it sit at room temperature for 30 minutes.

Scoop 2-tablespoon (45-gram) balls of the dough and set them on the prepared baking sheet about 1 inch apart (alternatively, use a bench scraper to cut and shape cookies by hand). Don't pat them down; they will spread as they bake. Sprinkle a little fleur de sel over each. Bake for 8 minutes, rotate the sheet, and bake for 5 minutes more, or until they turn a deep golden blond, and are firm around the edges and soft in the middle.

Let the cookies sit on the sheet for a few minutes before transferring to a wire rack to cool. Serve immediately or store in an airtight container.

Restaurant Index

FRIENDS & FAMILY 78
Hollywood
5150 Hollywood Boulevard
Los Angeles, CA 90004
friendsandfamilyla.com

GO GET EM TIGER 186
Larchmont
230 N. Larchmont Boulevard
Los Angeles, CA 90004
gandb.coffee

Los Feliz
4630 Hollywood Boulevard
Los Feliz, CA 90027

GRACIAS MADRE 31
West Hollywood
8905 Melrose Avenue
Los Angeles, CA 90069
graciasmadreweho.com

GREENSPAN'S GRILLED CHEESE 93
Beverly Grove
7461 Melrose Avenue
Los Angeles, CA 90046
greenspansgrilledcheese.com

GUELAGUETZA 164
Koreatown
3014 W. Olympic Boulevard
Los Angeles, CA 90006
ilovemole.com

HATCHET HALL 68
Culver City
12517 W. Washington Boulevard
Los Angeles, CA 90066
hatchethallla.com

HEIRLOOM L.A. 94
Eagle Rock
4120 Verdugo Road
Los Angeles, CA 90065
heirloomla.com

Cypress Park (Yolk & Flour)
3232 ½ N Figueroa Street
Los Angeles, CA 90065

HINOKI & THE BIRD 32
Beverly Hills
10 W. Century Drive
Los Angeles, CA 90067
hinokiandthebird.com

THE HUNGRY CAT 148
Hollywood
1525 N. Vine Street
Los Angeles, CA 90028
thehungrycat.com

JAR 183
Beverly Grove
8225 Beverly Boulevard
Los Angeles, CA 90048
thejar.com

JOAN'S ON THIRD 194
Beverly Grove
8350 W. 3rd Street
Los Angeles, CA 90048
joansonthird.com

Studio City
12059 Venutra Place
Studio City, CA 91604

JON & VINNY'S 223
Beverly Grove
412 N. Fairfax Avenue
Los Angeles, CA 90036
jonandvinnys.com

KALI 17
Larchmont
5722 Melrose Avenue
Los Angeles, CA 90038
kalirestaurant.com

L&E OYSTER BAR 145
Silverlake
1637 Silver Lake Boulevard
Los Angeles, CA 90026
leoysterbar.com

LA CASITA MEXICANA 157
Bell
4030 E. Gage Avenue
Bell, CA 90201
casitamex.com

LINCOLN 102
Pasadena
1992 Lincoln Avenue
Pasadena, CA 91103
lincolnpasadena.com

LITTLE DOM'S 200
Los Feliz
2128 Hillhurst Avenue
Los Angeles, CA 90027
littledoms.com

THE LITTLE DOOR 141
Beverly Grove
8164 W. 3rd Street
Los Angeles, CA 90048
thelittledoor.com

LITTLE FLOWER CANDY CO. 221
Pasadena
1424 W. Colorado Boulevard
Pasadena, CA 91105
littleflowercandyco.com

LOCAL KITCHEN + WINE BAR 41
Santa Monica
1736 Ocean Park Boulevard
Santa Monica, CA 90405
localkitchenandwinebar.com

LOCOL 65
Watts
1950 E. 103rd Street
Los Angeles, CA 90002
welocol.com

LOVE & SALT 123
South Bay
317 Manhattan Beach Boulevard
Manhattan Beach, CA 90266
loveandsaltla.com

LUCKY BOY 69
Pasadena
640 Arroyo Parkway
Pasadena, CA 91106
luckyboyburgers.com

M CAFÉ DE CHAYA 182
Beverly Grove
7119 Melrose Avenue
Los Angeles, CA 90046
mcafedechaya.com

Beverly Hills
9433 Brighton Way
Beverly Hills, CA 90210

M STREET KITCHEN 81
Santa Monica
2000 Main Street
Santa Monica, CA 90405
mstreetkitchen.com

MADCAPRA 42
DTLA
Grand Central Market
317 S. Broadway
Los Angeles, CA 90013
madcapra.com

MANHATTAN BEACH POST 59
South Bay
1142 Manhattan Avenue
Manhattan Beach, CA 90266
eatmbpost.com

MAPLE BLOCK MEAT CO. 110
Culver City
3973 Sepulveda Boulevard
Culver City, CA 90230
mapleblockmeat.com

MATSUHISA 147
Beverly Hills
129 N. La Cienega Boulevard
Beverly Hills, CA 90230
matsuhisabeverlyhills.com

MAURY'S BAGELS 72
Silverlake
2829 Bellevue Avenue
Los Angeles, CA 90026
maurysbagels.com

MCCALL'S MEAT & FISH CO. 211
Los Feliz
2117 Hillhurst Avenue
Los Angeles, CA 90027
mccallsmeatandfish.com

MEALS BY GENET 203
Beverly Grove
1053 S. Fairfax Avenue
Los Angeles, CA 90019
mealsbygenetla.com

MOON JUICE 55
Venice
507 Rose Avenue
Venice, CA 90291
moonjuiceshop.com

Silverlake
2389 Sunset Boulevard
Los Angeles, CA 90013

West Hollywood
8463-3 Melrose Place
Los Angeles, CA 90069

Restaurant Index CONTINUED

Index

(Page numbers in *italics* refer to illustrations.)

ACKNOWLEDGMENTS

If not for the generosity of so many L.A. restaurants and editor Jono Jarrett at Rizzoli for championing this project with such sincerity and humor, *The L.A. Cookbook* would not exist. Thank you to the infectiously enthusiastic and talented Noah Fecks for tackling an ambitious bicoastal shoot schedule; to Smog Design; to Nicki Clendening, also at Rizzoli; and to Sean Yashar of The Culture Creative. Special acknowledgment to Stuart Steingold for his guidance and Celia Steingold for her culinary mastery. I am grateful for the expertise and feedback of Gigi Jack, Grant Jack, and Marissa Steingold. Many thanks to Regina Connell, Heath Ceramics, Pauline Wolstencroft, and Jacqui Shine. Additional shout-outs to all the lovelies in food PR; Tony Konecny; and over at the test kitchen, to the palates of Chris Baker, David Dick, Melissa Goldstein, Eric Gross, RJ Kaufman, Tom Stevens, and Jackie Treitz.